ENTREPRENEURSHIP EDUCATION ENRICHES ENTREPRENEURIAL MANAGEMENT IN DIGITAL AGE

Dan Vivek Nathan, MBA, MSc, B.A, FCIM (U.K)

Author of *Global Market / Marketing Research in 21st Century and Beyond*

NEWMAN SPRINGS PUBLISHING
320 Broad Street
Red Bank, NJ 07701

First originally published by Newman Springs Publishing 2022

ISBN 978-1-68498-618-7 (Paperback)
ISBN 978-1-68498-620-0 (Hardcover)
ISBN 978-1-68498-619-4 (Digital)

Printed in the United States of America

CONTENTS

FOREWORD

As a college professor teaching Information Technology, I see no other time in history that has provided a better or more conducive opportunity for the self-discovery of entrepreneurship by all those aspiring to become successful entrepreneurs. Emerging technologies coupled with the outreach of the Internet have ushered in an era where entrepreneurship can bloom and thrive. This book written by the author is timely in that sense.

This book presents the core values, strengths, skillset, knowledge, and resources required for becoming an entrepreneur. The writing style makes for easy reading, and the flow of the content is logical, orderly, and well connected. The book is for anyone and everyone who dreams of becoming an entrepreneur. It can also serve as a self-help book for business executives as the scope of the book is broad and far-reaching.

The author appropriately starts with a chapter on self-discovery of oneself as an entrepreneur by pointing succinctly to the key traits of an entrepreneur. At the same time, he sheds light on the gender neutrality of entrepreneurship, a concept that resonates well with current times. Another compelling thrust of the book is that it takes a global view of entrepreneurship, reflecting a world that has recently opened for all to benefit from the sharing economy. With trade barriers easing and the Internet providing an expanded outreach to markets around the globe, the author with his international exposure, has taken a global view of entrepreneurship to a new level where the world now is the market for all.

Entrepreneurship can thrive in different forms in different companies, from small startups to large enterprises. The book acknowledges the differences and refrains from stressing a one solution fit-all narrative found in some other books. Categorizing and explaining entrepreneurship related to different business settings in the early chapters are intended as a foundation for understanding the different levels of entrepreneurship discussed subsequently in the book.

Yet another strength of the book is the focus on entrepreneurship education and the learning resources available. While the entrepreneurship spirit may be inherent in some, it is important to nurture it through education. Education gives structure and discipline to entrepreneurship. The book stresses the need for education, especially in today's digital world, where success in business can often depend on the discovery of knowledge, especially by grasping the role played by tools and technologies in the success of entrepreneurship.

The author presents a snapshot of cutting-edge technologies that can play a crucial role in putting entrepreneurs' skills into action. The listing of technologies such as Artificial Intelligence and others in the book provides insight into the emerging use of such technologies by entrepreneurs. Digital tools discussed in the subsequent chapter allow the contents to flow seamlessly from education to digital resources.

The book is also among a few that looks at managing entrepreneurship and managing a business as two different activities and provides excellent suggestions for both.

Understanding the distinction between the two activities as explained in the final chapters is essential for entrepreneurs to balance their effort between creativity and managing day-to-day operations.

The author is well-read gauging by the references listed and quoted. The author's propositions and conclusions on the subject are driven by the extensive reading of articles and published statistics. Some of the statistics presented in the book defy conventional wisdom, which adds value to the vision of entrepreneurship in the digital era. The statistics enhance and enrich the theme of the book. They substantiate conventional wisdom on entrepreneurship where they should and dispel them otherwise.

Overall, the book is well written as it addresses a trending topic by providing current and helpful information.

The author is aptly qualified academically and equally experienced practically to write a book on this subject. The book can be a self-help guide, a resource for information, or a guide for self-discovery as an entrepreneur. It should benefit entrepreneurial students, individuals, blooming entrepreneurs, and company executives in obtaining a broader perspective of entrepreneurship. The author must be commended for his writing style conducive to easy learning and grasping the subject. This book is a valuable addition to the literature on entrepreneurship.

Nanda Ganesan, PhD, Chair of Information Technology
Department, California State University, Los Angeles

PREFACE

For several decades, the field of *entrepreneurship* studies has been one of the most vibrant and expansive in business and management. Entrepreneurship and business ventures, start-ups, and SMEs (small and medium-sized enterprises) globally are now part and parcel of most mainstream businesses. Entrepreneurship is an important constituent of the infrastructure and functioning of business ventures, start-ups, and SMEs (small and medium-sized enterprises) and economies as it shapes social and economic stratification in an economy of a country and is an important vehicle of social mobility. Since the recognition of the importance of entrepreneurship and entrepreneurs, it has been widely accepted as a distinct field of study in the social sciences and business institutions across the globe. Entrepreneurship has played a vital role for over thousands of years as providers of needed services to the population, as well as a source of innovators. However, entrepreneurship has only been in the limelight in the civilized world in the last five decades that the global population and academic world have realized the important contribution to the economy to their respective countries, also to the "standard of living" in those countries. We see small and medium-sized enterprises (SMEs) dominate every country in every continent of the globe. However, the definition of what small and medium-sized enterprise (SME) or a business venture is varies by country. Small and medium-sized enterprises create new jobs and usually employ vast majority of a country's working population.

The objective of this book is to illuminate importance of entrepreneurship education that will distinctly enhance the entrepreneurial management in today's digital age. This book is particularly timely as a country's business ventures, start-ups, or SMEs are instrumental to economic development. Given the importance of business ventures /start-ups / SMEs to economic development, the author has recognized the need to increase the efficacy and efficiency of activities relevant to these enterprises. This book is meant for a wide spectrum of readers, including students and lecturers/professors, but more specifically for blooming entrepreneurs, would-be owners of small business ventures, and innovators who are exploring start-ups. This book is also a major step toward addressing the needs of entrepreneurship education as well as the entrepreneurial management in digital age. I have compiled seven chapters focusing on entrepreneurship from three perspectives, namely entrepreneurship education, entrepreneurial management, and entrepreneurial management in digital age.

Chapter 1 explains about *an entrepreneur* and qualities in order to be an entrepreneur and also enlightens the characteristics of an entrepreneur. The author describes the importance of entrepreneurs and their contribution toward the economic growth. The author also compares countries where men and women are entrepreneurs.

Chapter 2 offers various perspectives on entrepreneurship. The author considers the very core of entrepreneurship. He highlights business venture, start-up, and small and medium-sized enterprise (SME); and the objective is to help the reader understand what entrepreneurship is. It describes the importance of entrepreneurship with questions and the pursuit of opportunity in opening up a business venture or a start-up or a small and medium-sized enterprise (SME). This chapter explains the importance of business ventures, start-ups, and SMEs. The author highlights the concepts of innovation and creativity. There is an emphasis on global society to encourage and enlarge the entrepreneurship, especially among academics as they are the vehicle in a society. A list of countries where there is entrepreneurial spirit is mentioned in this chapter.

Chapter 3 underlines the different types of entrepreneurships. Chapters 4 and 5 focus on the importance of entrepreneurship education. These chapters provide valuable comprehensive discussion on how entrepreneurship education can be improved. Chapter 5 focuses on entrepreneurship education in colleges/universities around the world. In terms of entrepreneurship education, the author highlights on educational institutions around the world that are very much involved in teaching students.

Chapter 6 provides a comprehensive overview of the concept of entrepreneurial management. The author discusses the entrepreneurial management process. In this chapter, the author addresses the differences between the general management and entrepreneurial management. Specific attention is paid to inventory management, accounting management, and human resources management.

Chapter 7 highlights the entrepreneurial management in digital age that are crucial to the study of entrepreneurial management. The author focuses on the potential dynamism of entrepreneurial management in the digital age. This chapter furnishes how entrepreneurial management can gain benefits/advantages on the current digital technology. The author also discusses how digital technology and broadband-driven mobile/smartphone technologies support the business needs of business ventures, start-ups, and SMEs. He emphasizes the capabilities of digital technologies that would power the transformation of entrepreneurial management.

Most institutions in US, UK, and EU continually seek ways to improve and expand the entrepreneurship education offerings at their respective institutions. It is the author's hope that these chapters spur the reader's interest/passion in entrepreneurship and that the faculties in colleges/universities who are novice to entrepreneurship education will see an opportunity to embark into this field. The author hopes that lecturers/professors and students will pick up best practices as they work in entrepreneurial ventures and start-ups and the chapters will help them succeed.

CHAPTER 1

WHO IS AN ENTREPRENEUR?

An entrepreneur is a person (he/she) who tries to transform an idea into reality by utilizing available resources. The role of entrepreneur is very crucial; and he/she has the full power and authority in the business venture, start-up, or SME. An entrepreneur is also an individual (he/she) who undertakes self-directed initiatives and assumes personal risks in innovating/creating and operating a profit-oriented business. In other words, an entrepreneur, whether he or she, takes personal risk in pursuit of a new business, start-up, or small and medium-sized enterprise (SME); innovation; or even some other form of enterprise. There are four distinct categories of entrepreneurs, namely business ventures, start-ups, small and medium-sized enterprises (SMEs), and social entrepreneurs. An entrepreneur has to have the following *qualities* in order to become an entrepreneur:

- Foresight
- Search skills
- Self-confidence
- Imagination / creative ideas
- Practical knowledge

1

- Analytical ability
- Communication skill
- Organizational skill
- Computational skill

These qualities are, to some extent, innate. There are those that seem to lend themselves to enhancement through entrepreneurship education.

The following are the characteristics of an *entrepreneur*:

- Self-motivated/self-confident/optimist
- Passionate / creative or innovative / visionary
- Adaptable/flexible
- Team builder / possesses managerial skills
- Has the know-how in networking and the ability to network
- Has product/service knowledge

The creativity of the individual entrepreneur is magnified because a new business venture, start-up, or small and medium-sized enterprise (SME) can contribute significantly to economic growth and development of a country. Entrepreneurs are essential for economic development since they create capital/wealth/resources. When it comes to economic development, the role of entrepreneurs varies from country to country in terms of resources, industrial climate, and the political system prevailing in the country concerned to the growth of entrepreneurs. They are omnipresent in every country's economic system. Generally, entrepreneurs are individuals who notice opportunities and decide how to enlist the resources necessary to produce new and improved goods and services. In other words, entrepreneurs introduce new products or services into the market landscape, develop and implement new technologies, open new markets, discover new sources of supply, and recognize existing business ventures. They make all of the planning, organizing, and leading/delegating and control the decision-making process necessary to start new business ventures, start-ups, and small and medium-sized enterprises (SMEs).

Entrepreneurs require judgment and the know-how to identify combinations of market opportunities and the inventions' resources needed to achieve them. The characteristics of entrepreneurs are likely to be high on the personality trait of openness to experience. In brief, they are predisposed to be original, to be open to wide range of incitement, to be daring, and to take risks. They, too, are likely to have an internal locus of control. In short, they believe that they are responsible for what happens to them and that their own actions determine important outcomes, such as the success or failure of a new business venture, start-up, or small and medium-sized enterprise (SME). They are likely to have a high level of self-confidence and feel competent and capable of handling most situations, such as stress and the uncertainty surrounding a fall into a risky new venture, and also likely to have a high need for achievement and a strong desire to perform challenging tasks and meet high personal standards of excellence.

As the entrepreneur begins to realize the dream of owning a new business venture, start-up, or small and medium-sized enterprise (SME); opens the doors; and invites customers in, real work begins. He/she now handles all the administrative requirements of accounting, buying, selling, customer service, building maintenance, and other time-consuming necessities of enterprise ownership.

The term entrepreneur in German is *unternehmer* or *unternamer*, which, translated literally, means "undertaker." In France, where the term originated, the word *entrepredre* in French means "to undertake." Thus, the entrepreneur is an undertaker who undertakes to make things happen. In short, entrepreneurship is the ability to create and build something from practically nothing.

Usually entrepreneurs are action-oriented people who make decisions and undertake actions as they navigate ongoing enterprise activities, which leads to the accumulation of enormous experience. There are different types of entrepreneurs, each with a different personality types and attributes/behaviors such as

- innovator (with imaginative-ideas personality),
- new designer (with intuitive personality) and leader (with control as attribute),

3

- new entrepreneur (with opportunistic and risk-taking attribute), and
- adventurer (with energy as personality type).

Overall there are number of reasons for the parallel appeal and interest in entrepreneurship and creation of entrepreneurs across the globe. There are three primary reasons for it, which are job creation and economic development deregulation, and strategic realignment.

Globally there are about a billion of entrepreneurs. Nearly half a billion entrepreneurs are women who are impacting the global economy. An overwhelming majority of these women live in developing countries and have little education. They become entrepreneurs because of the following reasons: They have hobbies and passion and want to spend time working on it. The second reason is that, when they disengage their jobs, circumstances change so drastically that they need to start working for themselves. The third reason is that they cannot find jobs or need more income than what their current jobs provide.

In some countries such as Nigeria, Mexico, Thailand, Ghana, Ecuador, Panama, and Uganda, women take part in business at rates equal to men. In some countries such as Pakistan, they barely take part at all. A decade ago, Global Entrepreneurship Report gave the following statistics:

> The numbers below show the percentage of *men* and *women* entrepreneurs in a sampling of countries across the globe.

Comparison of Countries with Percentage of *Men* Entrepreneurs and Percentage of *Women* Entrepreneurs

	Men (percent)	Women (percent)
Belgium	4.3	2.0
Brazil	12.7	12.7
China	19.3	13.4
Hong Kong	14.3	5.8
India	9.5	7.5
Japan	3.5	5.2
Peru	25.7	26.1
Russia	3.8	1.6
UK	7.4	3.6
US	12.0	7.3

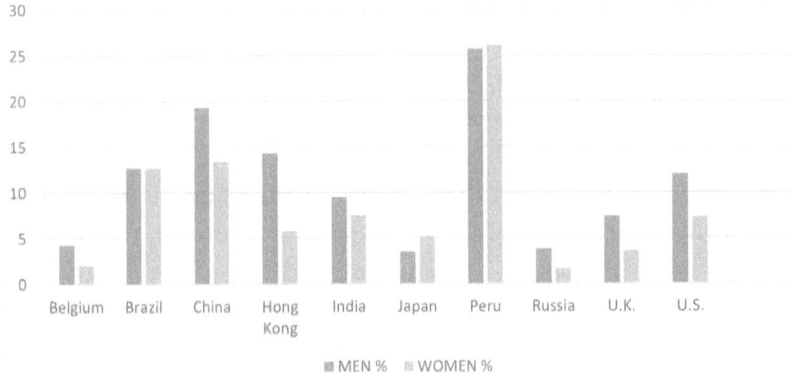

Comparison of countries with percentage of Men entrepreneurs and percentage of Women entrepreneurs

CHAPTER 2

ENTREPRENEURSHIP

What is entrepreneurship?

Entrepreneurship is the *process* through which individuals and teams bring together necessary resources to exploit opportunities and, in doing so, create wealth, social benefits, and prosperity. In other words, entrepreneurship is the process of designing, launching, and running a new business venture, start-up, or small and medium-sized enterprise (SME). It is also to develop, organize, and manage a business venture, start-up, or small and medium-sized enterprise (SME) with any risk to make a profit. Entrepreneurship is considered synonymous with start-up or other new creation of new business venture. Entrepreneurship refers to the concept of developing and managing a business venture in order to gain profit by taking risks. Entrepreneurship is a crucial element for economic progress as it manifests its fundamental importance in the following factors:

- By identifying, evaluating, and exploiting business opportunities
- By creating new business ventures, start-ups, and SMEs.

- By driving the economy of a country forward through *innovation* competence, creating jobs
- By improving the standard of living of a society

In layman's terms, the entrepreneurship process and business ventures, start-ups, and SMEs include several phases. The phases of the entrepreneurship process are as follows:

- **Innovation**
- **A trigger event**
- **Implementation**
- **Growth**
- **Maturity**

The entrepreneurship process begins with an *innovative idea* for a product/service. The time frame for the innovator(s) may be a month or even years before the entrepreneur moves on to the next phase. Usually a specific occurrence sparks the entrepreneur(s) to proceed further. Implementation is the phase of the entrepreneurship process in which the enterprise is formed. The entrepreneurial manager guides and nurtures the enterprise through the desired level and growth. The maturity phase of the enterprise is reached when the enterprise is considered well-established in the market landscape.

When it comes to *innovation*, we find there is the importance of *innovation* in entrepreneurship. This has been enlightened by coming up with new product(s)/service(s) to fulfill the ever-changing needs of the consumers/customers in the market landscape.

Entrepreneurship and entrepreneur are divided in three categories—the ones describing the role of entrepreneur, others describing the characteristics, and, the third category, the ones focusing on success factors. Therefore, an entrepreneur can be described as an individual (he/she) who carries out a role in the economic world by creating added value and who bears the risk and responsibility with a combination of specific personal characteristics (creative, innovative, and dynamic). The above conditions are vital to become an entrepreneur. *Entrepreneurship is a creative event* that can take place in a variety of settings. It is the capacity to view what others have overlooked and to act on the insight. It requires incredible know-how approach, which is focused on maximizing a particular cove that had previously gone unnoticed in the market landscape. In short, the essence of entrepreneurship is bringing about change that is beneficial in its result.

Entrepreneurship involves *innovation*, which is more than just having a good idea. In other words, it means perfecting and developing the idea and then implementing it in a business venture, start-up, or small and medium-sized enterprise (SME) or bringing it to the market landscape.

Often entrepreneurship is defined in terms of *innovation*, creativity, and willingness to take risk. *Innovation is entrepreneurship*. An innovative entrepreneur introduces commercial, scientific, and technological discoveries to the market landscape by incorporating them in new business ventures, start-ups, and small and medium-sized enterprises (SMEs). They not only furnish new products/services but also create new transaction methods, business institutions, and industries that fundamentally transform how the economy operates.

The innovative entrepreneur's impact on economic growth and development is voluminous and evident. In short, innovative entrepreneurs furnish a combination of inventions, initiative, and investment to the economy of a country. The innovative entrepreneur applies personal initiative to create the businesss venture, start-up, or small and medium-sized enterprise (SME), providing creativity, human capital, judgment, time and effort, and coordination. The innovative entrepreneur's investment in the business venture, start-up, or small and medium-sized enterprise (SME) is usually funded by personal income and wealth, contribution from friends and relatives, and outside sources such as venture capital and bank loans.

Innovation is always associated with increase in productivity that lower the cost of human resources required for products/services. In brief, *innovation* plays a significant role in determining the business venture, start-up, or SME growth. The reigning concept is that entrepreneurship and *innovation* are strongly associated with business venture, start-ups, and SMEs. But there is a positive effect among enterprises' growth; and *innovation* owing to market, characteristics of business venture, start-ups, and SMEs and geographical environment. In essence, innovation is the process by which individuals, on their own or within their companies, pursue opportunities without regard to resources available.

Innovation and entrepreneurship are interrelated as it comprised of independent business efforts in assembling and deploying resources in capturing the value in *innovative products or services*. Entrepreneurship is a mental attitude / behavior of an individual.

Innovation is the final step in the creative process, which sees the idea from its beginning through its incubation into its adoption.

We see there is an enormous talent in *entrepreneurship* in the world. Entrepreneurship is a permanent concern in almost all developed countries. The economic leaders of these developed countries insist on the importance of promoting the entrepreneurial spirit in young individuals in order to encourage the setting up of new business ventures, start-ups, and small and medium-sized enterprises (SMEs). Although a small number of individuals become entrepreneurs, there is a significantly larger number who could be the creative change makers around the globe. Creating a new business venture, start-up, or small and medium-sized enterprise (SME) is a complex process involving different elements, in particular the different factors which constitute the profile of the individual entrepreneur. Entrepreneurship is more than a set of tools/techniques for start-ups or rather starting a new business venture. It is a *mindset*, a way of looking at things that is opportunity focused on creative. In other words, it is about passion, doing what he/she loves to pursue. Entrepreneurship is also about creating wealth in terms of money resources, independence, power, and *innovation* and also about challenge and persistence. In brief, it is for those who are self-motivated, independent, and persistent; have a sense of humor; can learn and bounce back from failure; and are willing to take and manage calculated risks.

Entrepreneurship is a process during which a certain number of risks are taken, and successful entrepreneurs have a wide range of skills and personal characteristics. The characteristics of entrepreneurship can be taught, and these need to be developed by means of *entrepreneurship education programs*. In short, *entrepreneurship education* should be placed on the skills needed to spot business opportunities and assess their feasibility.

The word *entrepreneurship* is exciting, and it can call up images of successful business tycoons. It is a vital part of the structure and functioning of business/firms and economies. Entrepreneurship can also shape social and economic stratification in an economy and may be a crucial vehicle of social mobility. For the past several decades, entrepreneurship has been the engine that has driven the global economy in good times and the life vest that has kept it afloat during upheaval. It has been in the last two decades that the general public and the academic world have come to realize the important contribution toward the economy and standard living those entrepreneurs make. It is important to the undergoing economic success of every nation in the world.

Global society must find ways to encourage and enlarge the entrepreneurial spirit, and the colleges/universities are the principal vehicle in a society by which encouragement can be done. The fact of the matter is essential economic decisions of what, how, and for whom are totally decided by the lecturer/professor, who perform the same role as the planner in a common economy. So whether the country is developed or underdeveloped, or third-world country for that matter, the institution can play an essential role. In brief, this can be done by *creating a new entrepreneurial educational environment* in which the creative divergent traits of the entrepreneurial spirit are encouraged and enhanced. The classroom / lecture room environment needs to be reformed if entrepreneurship education is to be encouraged.

Entrepreneurship is traditionally associated with a particular form of business venture activity, the creation of a business/company. In developed countries, entrepreneurship is the symbol of business tenacity and achievement. Entrepreneurs in developed countries have been the pioneers of entrepreneurial successes due to their innovative talents and their capacity for accomplishment. They will continue to be critical contributors to economic growth through their leadership, management, innovative ideas, research capabilities and development effectiveness, job creation, competitiveness, productivity, and formation of new business ventures. In emerging markets, entrepreneurs shape the formal sector; establish business ventures, start-ups, and small and medium-sized enterprises (SMEs); create markets for goods, services, labor, and finance; and build basic industries. In brief, innovative entrepreneurs and economic growth are mutually reinforcing.

Global Entrepreneurship Report indicated the following countries with entrepreneurial spirit in the twenty-first century:

Rank	Country
1	Denmark
2	Canada
3	United States
4	Sweden
5	New Zealand
6	Ireland
7	Switzerland
8	Norway
9	Iceland
10	Netherlands
11	Australia
12	Belgium
13	Finland
14	United Kingdom
15	Singapore
16	Germany
17	Puerto Rico
18	France
19	Slovenia
20	South Korea

21	Israel
22	Austria
23	Hong Kong
24	UAR
25	Czech Republic

Below is a ranking of how easy an entrepreneur can start a *business venture* based on the procedures, time, costs, and capital requirements that governments impose:

Overall Rankings

Rank	Country
1	Singapore
2	New Zealand
3	United States
4	United Kingdom
5	Denmark
6	Ireland
7	Canada
8	Australia
9	Norway

Business ventures, start-ups, small and medium-sized enterprises (SMEs) are at the heart of our world and are the driving force of local economic development. With all of the start-up economies, when you really think about it, the world is one big start-up ecosystem. It is about people helping people and about creating and being the change they wish to see in the world. In developed countries, the number of newly started start-up companies is relatively high, and these companies contribute to new jobs as well as to the dynamics and development of industries and economies. These newly established companies constitute an important proportion of the business stock in an economy, and they are thereby also important for employment.

There are many individuals with ambitions to start a business venture. They are widespread in the populations around the world who would like to pursue a business venture. But they don't have enough financial resources to start a business venture. Financial resources refer to the property, stocks and bonds, tangible goods, and other assets that can be pledged in exchange for credit or money used in leasing or purchasing resources. These financial resources are critical for entrepreneurship. The primary reason that business start-ups require a substantial sum of money and that entrepreneurs' access to credit markets is constrained is due to risks associated with new business ventures.

Business venture

Business venture is a new business that is formed with a plan and expectations that financial gain will follow. It is typically a small business beginning with a small number of financial resources. It is usually formed out of a need for a product/service that is lacking in the market landscape. As the business venture gets off its ground, additional investors may get involved by furnishing support and capital to expand development of the venture. In other words, entrepreneurs usually seek to achieve a certain goal by opening up a new business venture that will address the needs of society and market landscape. Entrepreneurs around the globe have a major role in creating new business ventures for economic growth. In other words, they strive to make a difference in the world and contribute to its betterment.

In the twenty-first century, they utilize a combination of *innovation* and digital technologies to encourage effective means of activity in life. The business venture team creates a road map of plan that can lead to the commercialization of the new products/services in the market landscape. Business venture environment with sound infrastructure and legal protections will encourage entrepreneurs.

Entrepreneurs of business ventures boom in countries that provide legal and social incentives for their activities.

Entrepreneurship is more than the spawning of a business venture and the wealth that associates with it. It is focused on the creation of a new business venture that serves society and makes a positive change. In their journey of entrepreneurship, they encounter obstacles. But they are prepared to respond to challenge to overcome obstacles/problems and build a business venture. In other words, when they encounter difficult situations, they are prepared to make the extra effort to overcome those obstacles and succeed.

Countries around the World by Measures of *Economic Activity*

Country	Business Environment	Business Venture Index
US	1	1
Netherlands	2	4
UK	3	3
Germany	8	8
Switzerland	4	7
Finland	5	2
Sweden	7	5
France	9	9
Japan	10	10
Ireland	6	6

Start-up

Start-up is defined as a new business enterprise that is subject to the entrepreneur's financial and liquidity constraints. The start-up becomes a company when it no longer is subject to the entrepreneur's financial and liquidity constraints. The entrepreneur creates a start-up as an instrument to establish a company. Entrepreneurs raise additional investment at some/several growth stages of the company.

In short, start-up is a company undertaken by an entrepreneur to seek, develop, and validate a scalable model. Start-up investing is the action of making an investment of the founder's own contribution of financial resources in an initial phase of the company. Entrepreneurs raise additional investment at some or several growth phases of the company. In other words, entrepreneurs in start-ups are founders involved in the initial launch of start-ups. These founders of start-ups are responsible for their overall strategies of the start-ups. They play the role of chief executive officer of a company. Many colleges/universities offer training on start-ups. These institutions conduct courses/programs in entrepreneurship that deal with topic of start-ups.

Start-up usually is an entrepreneurial venture rather than a young starter company founded by one or more individual entrepreneurs to develop a unique product/service and bring it to the market landscape. One of the initial tasks is to raise enough money to further develop the product/service. At the initial stage, start-ups face high uncertainty and have high rates of failure. Start-up entrepreneurs often become too certain about their start-ups and their influence on an outcome. In short, entrepreneurs tend to believe they have more degree of control over events discounting the role of luck. Many entrepreneurs seek feedback from experienced or more knowledgeable individuals to guide them in creating their start-ups.

Small and medium-sized enterprise (SME)

The definition of SMEs (small and medium-sized enterprises) varies by country and, in some countries, by industry sector. The acronym SME originated in Europe. SMEs play an important role in the economy of a country, employing vast number of people and helping to shape *innovation*. In other words, small and medium-sized enterprises (SMEs) are important for economic and social reasons, given the sector's role in employment. In any country's national economy, SMEs sometimes outnumber large companies by a wide margin and also employ numerous people.

Though they do not have the reasons of large companies, their vital element is entrepreneurial; and therefore, they are crucial to *innovation* and growth of a country's economy. In brief, SMEs are identified by the number of people they employ; and in some cases, they measure by revenues/sales. For example, in Canada, SMEs refer to business with fewer than five hundred employees and less than fifty million dollars in gross revenues.

SMEs contribute to economic growth in several ways:

- SMEs foster radical *innovation*.
- SMEs contribute more opportunities for economic growth.

SMEs can often be more flexible and responsive to customer needs than large companies. If the size of SME is smaller, then the ability to respond to changes and achieve deeper and closer interaction among the consumers/customers such as

- deeper consumer/customer knowledge,
- faster decision making,
- increased employee interaction,
- participation in planning activities, and
- vested interest in business success.

Furthermore, the advent of current Internet technologies, e-commerce, offers considerable opportunities to SMEs to expand their customer base, enter new product/service markets, and rationalize their businesses.

Entrepreneurship is crucial to breaking the sinful cycle of neediness and dependency that has inflamed countries in Africa, Asia, and Latin America. These countries have enormous potential of economic growth because there are many natural resources and unused opportunities available in those countries. An abundance of natural resources does not ensure economic growth and development in these countries. The economic growth is largely a function of human creativity, drive, and willingness to sacrifice, the very attributes that lie at the heart of entrepreneurship. The two most vital characteristics of entrepreneurship as it affects economic growth and development are the entrepreneur's ability to see an opportunity overlooked by others and the entrepreneur's ability to develop the opportunity with the appropriate level of *innovation*. In executing these two functions, the entrepreneur's contribution results in the creation of new markets and new demands of new supplies. This, in turn, expands employment opportunities and creates secondary benefits because of the multiplier effect in the economy of a country.

Entrepreneurship is a matter of behavior of individuals or organizations. Entrepreneurship is also a matter of specific situations such as creation of new businesses and acquiring existing businesses, corporate venturing, etc. More than four decades ago, entrepreneurship has emerged as a vital element in the dynamics of modern economics. Since then, small and medium-sized enterprises (SMEs) have become the major source of new job creators.

Over the last three decades, there has been an unprecedented increase of the number of entrepreneurs who start their own business ventures, start-ups, or small and medium-sized enterprises (SMEs) in developed countries. This level of growth coincides with the market demand and opportunities seen in software applications industry. In 2020, individuals and start-ups have made major contribution to the discovery of new technologies and to their commercial applications. Business venture creation and the encouragement of an entrepreneurial culture have become fundamental topics among economists, academics, and politicians in almost all countries around the world. In short, this interest is based upon existing evidence that new business ventures contribute to creation of jobs, social and political stability, *innovation*, and economic development.

If an individual (he/she) wants to start up a new business venture, he or she should have to ask himself or herself the following questions:

- Why is your start-up / new business venture different from others? This question is to evaluate your business potential to create barriers of entry for competitors.
- What type of start-up / new business venture do you want to build? This will impact what kind of team you build and funding for the business etc.

- What is the name of your start-up / new business venture?
- What makes you *unique* as an entrepreneur?
- What is your business *idea*?
- Define and refine your solution. How can your *idea* be different and valuable to your customers you would cater?
- Understand the opportunity and market.
- Write out one or two products/services that your start-up / new business venture will offer to customers.
- Now that you have begun to build the *foundation*, next phase is building core values and building culture.
- Now it's very important to find a *team* with the right mix.
- Write your *brand*.
- Begin *funding*.
- Craft a marketing program.
- Focus your efforts on building a sales engine.
- Make continuous *innovation* integration to your start-up / new business venture.

CHAPTER 3

TYPES OF ENTREPRENEURSHIPS

As stated in the previous chapter, entrepreneurship is the dynamic process of identifying economic opportunities and starting a business venture, start-up, SME, or other enterprises in the market landscape. The entrepreneur (he/she) develops a business prototype and obtains the required resources, including human resources. It's about taking risks and can be either a success or a failure. In brief, entrepreneurship is the process of launching and running a business. It is the purposeful and organized search for change conducted after systematic analysis of opportunities in the market landscape. Business ventures, start-ups, and SMEs make indispensable contribution to the market economics. They are an essential part of the renewal processes that encompasses and defines the market economies. In fact, they play an immense role in the *innovation* that led to technological change and productivity growth. Entrepreneurs usually have different aspirations and visions for the type of business venture, start-up, or SME they wish to create. As a social and economic episode, entrepreneurship has been regarded as an engine of economic development and renewal; transformation and growth; a way to create jobs; a way to organize business ventures, start-ups, SMEs; a set of individual skills; and a way of being and learning.

Entrepreneurship can be considered as an academic subject. In other words, we are educated on what entrepreneurship is taught as, how it is taught, and the reasons for teaching this subject in colleges and universities. . It impacts our understanding of what entrepreneurship is. Entrepreneurs create jobs, and in turn, they make contribution to the economy. We find there are several categories of entrepreneurs, namely the following:

- Small-business entrepreneur
- Start-up entrepreneur
- Innovative entrepreneur
- Large-company entrepreneur
- Social entrepreneur
- Buyer entrepreneur
- Hustler entrepreneur
- Imitator entrepreneur
- Research entrepreneur

Each of these entrepreneur categories tends to choose according to their abilities, personality, and environment in the market landscape. They have their own rules and regulations to adhere for their enterprises' success. Each leader of these enterprises has to have certain topmost qualities.

Top qualities of an entrepreneurial leader percentagewise

- Vision—77 percent
- Passion—74 percent
- Integrity—55 percent
- Innovation—50 percent
- Risk-taker—47 percent
- Resilience—45 percent
- Proactiveness—43 percent
- Relentless customer focus—40 percent

- Ability to learn—38 percent
- Flexibility—35 percent

Entrepreneurship occurs when enterprising individuals (he/she) pursue profitable opportunities. There are several categories of entrepreneurship. They are as follows.

Small-business entrepreneur

Small-business entrepreneur is often an individual (he/she) who owns and operates their own business. They usually hire local employees or keep family to run their business.

Examples are local groceries, corner shops, and restaurants.

Start-up entrepreneur

This type of entrepreneur has an eye to identify needs in the market landscape and furnish adequate solutions as a business idea. In other words, they look for things that are not available in the marketplace and create solutions for them. Their vision is to find a business prototype that is scalable in market landscape. Most of start-ups are usually technology focused.

Examples are Uber and Instagram.

Innovative entrepreneur

This type of entrepreneur develops entirely with new ideas and turn them into viable business opportunities. They are deeply motivated because of their business ideas. They attract investors fairly easy. The ability of this type of entrepreneur is to make their products/services stand out from their competitors. They are constantly designing/developing new inventions. They find ways to make their products/services stand out from others in the marketplace.

Examples are Microsoft and Apple.

Large-company entrepreneur

Large companies are for professionals who know how to sustain innovation. They create new products/services based on consumer preference to meet market demand.

Examples are Intel and Amazon.

Social entrepreneur

Social entrepreneurs are individuals who pursue initiatives and opportunities to address social problems and needs in order to improve society and well-being, such as reducing poverty level, increasing literacy rate, protecting the natural environment, or reducing drug abuse. Social entrepreneurs solve social problems with their products/services. They are usually nonprofit companies dedicated toward social goal.

Examples are Muhammad Yunus and Grameen Bank.

Buyer entrepreneur

They utilize their money resource for the business ventures. Their objective is to grow and expand their business ventures.

An example is Berkshire Hathaway.

Hustler entrepreneurs

A hustler entrepreneur is someone who does work and puts in more effort. In other words, they are willing to work hard. They often start on small scale and grow big. They possess amazing work ethic.

An example is Mary Kay Cosmetics.

Imitator entrepreneur

This type of entrepreneur doesn't invent anything new. They use others' business ideas in products/services and work to improve them.

An example is Walmart.

Research entrepreneur

They do research before offering a product/service. They have deep understanding of the needs of their customers/consumers of their market landscape. When an individual has an idea, they do adequate research to collect relevant information because they believe a business has a higher chance of success.

Examples are Oracle and Lego.

The abovementioned entrepreneurs have got to have *management skills* and *personal characteristics* to be successful in the entrepreneurial life.

The following *management skills* are considered as essential for successful entrepreneurs of business ventures, start-ups, and SMEs:

- Plan the enterprise prior to establishing it—Planning is taught in *entrepreneurship education* in most of the schools/colleges/universities. The advantage of learning *business planning* is as follows:
    1. Entrepreneurs tend to make fewer mistakes, and this can be identified in the planning phase.
    2. Entrepreneurs are obliged to address all the important factors of the planned enterprise.
    3. Future-oriented action can be taken into consideration.
    4. Business planning phase is an ideal opportunity for testing ideas.
- Have management skills and use professional experts or advisers or consultants when necessary.
- Entrepreneurs must have good human relations with needs of their consumers/customers.
- Knowledge of their competitors—Entrepreneurs must know who their competitors are and their market share, strengths, and weaknesses in the market landscape.
- Entrepreneurs have got to know their target market's requirements and needs and how to meet these needs.
- Realize the importance of quality of the products/services.

- Entrepreneurs have got to know the accounting systems.

Entrepreneurs possess specific personal characteristics in respect of the enterprise they run. The following personal characteristics are considered as vital for successful entrepreneurs of business ventures, start-ups, and SMEs:

- Steadfastness/perseverance—Entrepreneurs are usually confident in themselves and their enterprises and persevere despite setbacks and difficult encounters. They can make immediate decisions but have enough patience to complete a task and attain an objective. They do not lose confidence when they make mistakes.
- Commitment to their business venture, start-up, or SME— Entrepreneurs give everything to establish and build the enterprise. They prove their commitment by using their personal funds in the enterprise, working long hours to achieve success in their business.
- Involvement in business venture, start-up, or SME— Entrepreneurs are personally involved in their enterprises and know what is happening at all levels and in all departments of the enterprise.
- Willingness to take risks—Entrepreneurs are usually trying to avoid unnecessary risks by using opportunities to spread risk.
- Good consumer/customer relations—Entrepreneurs have got to have good relationship with their consumers/customers. They should motivate their employees to build up contacts to benefit the enterprise.
- Creative and innovative—This helps them to compete with their competitors.
- Positive attitude and approach—These important personal characteristics are considered an essential for entrepreneurial life.

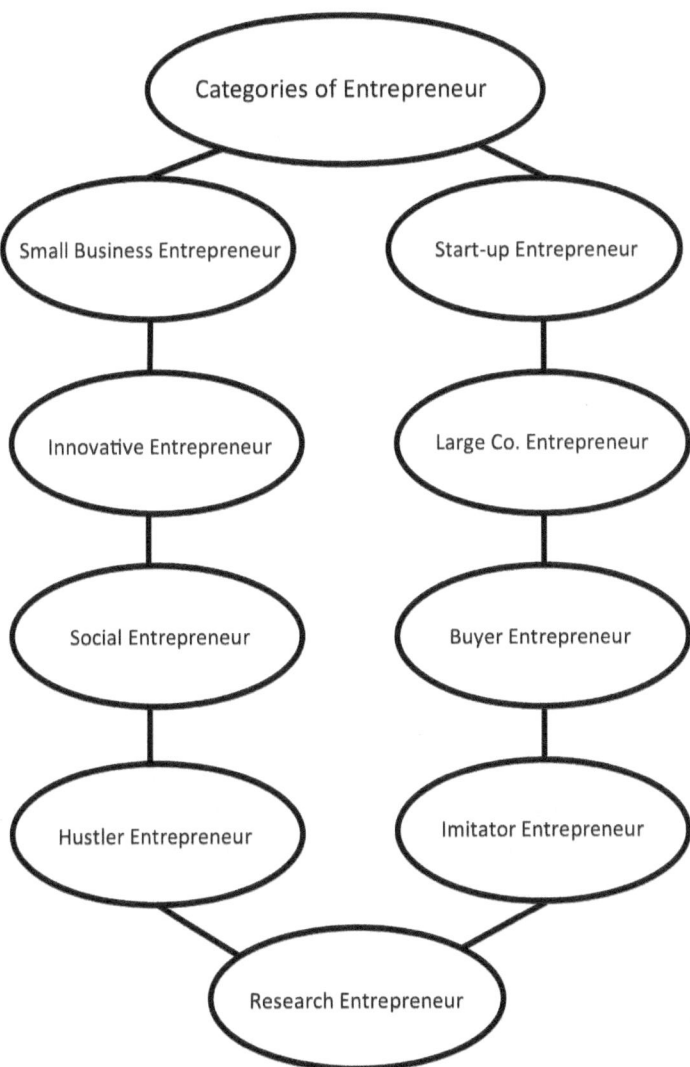

Fig: 1 Different types of Entrepreneurs

CHAPTER 4

ENTREPRENEURSHIP EDUCATION

Entrepreneurship education has experienced remarkable growth over the past several decades. It has become a type of umbrella for the analytical, social, leadership, and *innovative* skills that entrepreneurs rely on to achieve their success in business. Entrepreneurship education derives its importance from several factors, such as demand among students for information in entrepreneurship, need to furnish students with entrepreneurship skills related to making jobs, and need for economic growth through job creation.

To furnish students with entrepreneurial skills, entrepreneurship education must focus on the following attributes:

- Identification of market opportunity
- The generation of business idea to address the opportunity
- Commitment of resources to pursue the opportunity in the face of risk
- Creation of an operating business venture, start-up, or SME to implement the idea

Entrepreneurship education seeks to furnish students with the knowledge, skills, and motivation to encourage entrepreneurial success in a variety of settings. In brief, entrepreneurship education focuses on the development of skills that enable the realization of opportunity, where management is focused on the best way to operate. Entrepreneurship education has taken on some of the characteristics of an empowered academic field, and a number of courses and programs are currently being offered. Entrepreneurship education programs/courses are increasingly being taught in effort to equip students with the know-how and competency necessary to create economic value and jobs.

Most of the universities furnish opportunities to interact with entrepreneurs that serve as role models, design business plans, and have the business skills and also award *innovative* ideas. Many universities have offered an increasing number of institutional programs/ courses dedicated to entrepreneurship culture and development in undergraduate level as well as graduate level. In other words, the popularity of entrepreneurship programs/courses has increased dramatically among both undergraduate and graduate students. Moreover, alumni and external constituencies of business schools have been supportive of the development of entrepreneurship programs/ courses. The demand and supply of entrepreneurship lecturers/professors have increased. In universities, research on entrepreneurship and entrepreneurship education are being performed. Even globally students demand for entrepreneurship education, and entrepreneurial management courses/programs are currently in high demand according to OECD (Organization for Economic Cooperation and Development).

Several years ago, resistance to entrepreneurship education existed among lecturers/professors and administrators rather than among students. The academic impact on entrepreneurship education and entrepreneurial management are likely to remain high in years to come. More than four decades ago, the academic world recognized the importance of entrepreneurship education for economic development of a country. Since then, there has been an increasing attention given to the teaching of entrepreneurship in colleges and universities in developed as well as in developing countries. In short, over the past two decades, demand for entrepreneurship education programs and courses has skyrocketed.

In the early years of entrepreneurship education, teachers, lecturers, and professors tried to teach the courses/programs in the best way possible way to students. Currently a body of knowledge has been designed and developed that provides the beginning of a theoretical framework for the teaching of entrepreneurship. In developed countries, economic leaders and government authorities insist on the importance of encouraging the entrepreneurial spirit in young men and women in order to encourage the setting up of business ventures. Entrepreneurship is traditionally associated with a particular form of business activity—the creation of a new business venture. Therefore, entrepreneurship education must be directed toward stimulating entrepreneurship in the form of new-business-venture creation. Many business schools/universities have incorporated the practice of business creation into their entrepreneurship education curriculum.

Traditionally colleges/universities are involved in educating students the core of entrepreneurship. Many decades ago, entrepreneurship education at college/university level has evolved from courses in small-business management to full-scale curriculum at many colleges/universities in developed countries. Entrepreneurship education in colleges/universities have so far been developed as an add-on to business education, first as an elective course, then more courses/programs, and finally as a concentration of major program.

Most colleges/universities now offer one or more courses/programs related to entrepreneurship or small-business management, introduction to management (business plan development), financial management (financial aspect), marketing management, human resources management (staffing), and tax management. These courses appeal to students, and their interest is rising. We find that the skills traditionally taught in colleges/universities in developed as well as in developing countries are vitally important but not sufficient enough to make a successful entrepreneur. The colleges/universities have got to introduce various models and programs/courses specifically designed to develop in entrepreneurship students the insights and characteristics of the entrepreneur. They need to include the following skills:

- Communication skills (for example, persuasion skills)
- Creativity skills
- Leadership skills
- Negotiating skills
- Problem-solving skills
- Social-networking skills
- Time management skills

Since entrepreneurs can come from all walks of life, increasingly attention has to be made, focusing on academic entrepreneurs, social entrepreneurs, and technical entrepreneurs, among others. If colleges/universities are to maintain their leading role and lecturers/professors are to assist and facilitate new market and its support system, the choice to infuse entrepreneurship education in colleges/universities rest with each individual lecturer/professor. It means activities on *entrepreneurship* along with regular curriculums. A major plan for encouraging infusion is for lecturers/professors to conduct workshops, seminars, webinars.

There are many means of teaching entrepreneurship, such as lectures, case studies, discussions, films, videos, role plays, and simulation. Utilizing these vehicles, entrepreneurship students can read about, view, and try to imagine the real world from their own lecture rooms. However, on-the-screen participation furnishes the very best means of learning about specific concepts, skills, and values.

Entrepreneurship education can provide the following benefits:

- Career planning (entrepreneurship students have to understand the unlimited options of starting a business venture)
- Basic economic awareness
- Business understanding (to understand all business functions)
- Business planning
- Application of skills

- Community understanding (to gain an understanding of the suppliers available and to analyze the demographic that will affect the success of chosen business venture)
- Self-understanding and orientation to change (to look for changes that may lead to business opportunities of the future)
- Creativity (it encourages all kinds of innovative thinking related to new products/services, changes in demographics, new technology, social change, and community needs)
- Business management
- Business decision making

The most valuable economic resource lies in the knowledge, skills, and attitudes of workforce, present and future. Entrepreneurship education is a vehicle for higher education that brings new prospects and challenges. Entrepreneurship education is to make significant impact on global entrepreneurial attitudes of students in colleges/universities. It will depend on the attitudes of each lecturer/professor in their institutions.

Entrepreneurship education should focus on the following:

- Developing innovation
- Risk taking
- Imagination and problem-solving skills
- Decision-making skills

These specialized skills can be designed and developed through active courses/programs in consultation with local entrepreneurs as well as experts in the field. The students of entrepreneurship education should also be presented with open-ended situations that require them to work through problems and situations with changing conditions. Through this process, students of entrepreneurship will develop skills in adapting to new information and making decisions with imperfect knowledge. Critical thinking and assessment skills will also be developed.

In the past, the role played by small and medium-sized enter-prises in the economic and social welfare of many societies have become incontestable because of the fact that small and medium-sized business venture accounts for the majority of newly created jobs are now largely acceptable. It has been widely recognized that small and medium-sized enterprises (SMEs), as well as the establishment of new business ventures and start-ups, play a vital role in any econ-omy. In twenty-first century, expectations on small business ventures, start-ups, small and medium-sized enterprises (SMEs) as creators of employment and reorganizers of the economy are extremely strong. In developed countries, colleges/universities understand as a social system that it becomes entrepreneurial as members of faculty, stu-dents, and employees turn themselves somehow into entrepreneurs.

Entrepreneurship and entrepreneurship education have become more evident since the end of the twentieth century due to the increasing impact of entrepreneurship and small business ventures phenomenon on countries. In most colleges/universities in Western countries, entrepreneurship programs provide opportunities for stu-dents of entrepreneurship education to consult with small business ventures. There are two types of entrepreneurship programs cur-rently being followed in colleges/universities in Western countries. The first type is the *composite model* in which a series of courses/programs are taught out of traditional academic departments. This includes courses/programs in small business management, taxation, finance, and computing for small business ventures. The other model is known as *integrated model*. This is delivered through a separate department or center for entrepreneurial studies in colleges and universities.

There is a fundamental difference between small business man-agement courses and entrepreneurship education. Small business management is a very narrow field that provides instruction on how to run a small business. Entrepreneurship education includes small business management as well as the steps necessary to innovate, start a business venture, and carry it forward. We find that small busi-ness management course/program is one which concentrates on the starting of a small business venture, its operations, and its problems whereas entrepreneurship course is one which focuses on entrepreneurs as individuals and their role in business venture and society. Entrepreneur courses/programs are also concerned with *innovation* and new business venture rather than management of a business venture.

Entrepreneurship is a topic that can be integrated into the secondary / high school education level in a variety of courses. Integrating entrepreneurship into the secondary / high school curriculum begins with awareness. In other words, students need to be aware of the importance of entrepreneurship in the economy and of the possibility of entrepreneurship as a career choice for themselves.

At the college/university level in Western countries, entrepreneurship education has not only grown exponentially but has also changed dramatically over the past four decades. They stress the need of students of entrepreneurship education to prepare a lengthy and detailed business plan and also focus on business venture feasibility study. In other words, students have got to learn the entrepreneurial process, opportunity recognition, entry strategies, market opportunities and marketing, creating a successful business plan, financial projections, venture capital, debt and other forms of financing, external assistance for start-ups and small business venture, legal and tax issues, intellectual property, franchising, and entrepreneurship economics.

They also see entrepreneurship education as a multidisciplinary study, which includes psychology, sociology, and political science as these subjects provide vital insights that the entrepreneur needs to have communicated during the educational process.

Entrepreneurship education furnishes students with the know-how of business skills and motivates to encourage success in business ventures. In other words, it focuses on the development of essential business skills that enable the realization of opportunity where management education, human resources, marketing, operations, and accounting/ finance are focused on the best way to operate a business venture. Entrepreneurship education is often centered on improving the students' ability to write a *business plan*. Entrepreneurship students should be taught the formulation of their potential business idea by going through a number of stages such as problem recognition including problem description, information gathering and problem analysis, and formulation and evaluation of alternatives as well as implementation. In the *business plan*, students have got to define *their business*, describe their management team and organizational structure of business venture, describe the market, decide on a marketing plan and a business system, and choose how to implement their business idea with respect to finance, risks, and cash flow.

Besides entrepreneurship education in colleges/universities, communities have got to encourage entrepreneurs to launch new ventures, and training and management education will keep enterprises viable. We find there is an enormous growth of entrepreneurship in restaurants / food services, transportation, real estate, tax and financial services, computing, etc. Communities and government bodies should encourage training for entrepreneurship business skills, accounting, and basic law and management.

Points to consider in designing and developing worldwide entrepreneurship education

- Incorporate entrepreneurship education into all levels of education. In other words, to keep the entrepreneurship education program at colleges/universities dynamic and proactive so as to meet continued challenges, entrepreneurship education must be at the forefront of leadership development.
- Develop courses/programs that offer long-term education as well as short-term education and training for current and future start-up and business venture entrepreneurs.
- Present entrepreneurship education as a career option for college/university students. Entrepreneurial skills can be included in new expanded programs/courses or infused into the curriculum through the following areas:
  - Business/office education
  - Health field
  - Marketing

- Agriculture and so forth
- Develop a multi-optional delivery systems such as home study, TV, Internet/online, etc. Guidelines can be developed to provide effective and efficient entrepreneurship education.
- Develop networks through new communication technologies to deliver educational offerings via distance learning, video materials, etc.
- Design and develop small business training with necessary business and technical skills such as management, human resources, marketing, accounting, finance, etc.
- Develop skills which include the needed competencies for start-ups. These skills would enable one to determine entrepreneurship potential, the market opportunities for development, and funding possibilities.
- Provide evaluating tools for the entrepreneur and collaborate with diverse sectors to promote successful business ventures. For the start-up entrepreneur, a self-analysis of potential qualifications is vital, and this evaluation can show the additional preparation for entrepreneurship education and training that may be needed and will indicate whether or not an individual (he/she) should attempt a business venture.
- Furnish support management.
- Develop human resources for the business venture. In other words, entrepreneurship education with available resources will fill a need for human resource development.
- Consider workshops and webinars that can be offered in entrepreneurial skills, entrepreneurship leadership training, sharing resources, and exchanging ideas. The exchange of ideas and information will strengthen the role of all groups.
- Provide training for entrepreneurship educators with new developments in entrepreneurship education and the use of new skills such as internet technologies etc. These training can be offered through colleges/universities.
- Encourage research on entrepreneurship education.

The goals of entrepreneurship education to students can be in a broad range of subjects varying from the acquirement of specific know-how on the business venture, start-up, or SME and entrepreneurial management of new enterprises through the identification and simulation of entrepreneurial skills to the creation of an awareness of the procedure involved in the initiation and entrepreneurial management of an enterprise.

The following topics can be dealt with students in entrepreneurship education curriculum in colleges/universities:

- For business venture, start-up, and SME—creativity, obtaining the required resources, financing new ventures, planning new ventures, identification and evaluation of opportunities, implementation of new ventures, starting new ventures, risk analysis, and entrepreneurial management of new ventures
- Marketing—brand management, marketing planning, marketing strategy, entrepreneurial marketing, product/service development, and marketing of new product/service
- Financial aspects—accounting, financial planning, cash flow analysis, financing growing ventures, development of budget control system, valuation of a venture, and financial analysis
- Human resources management—enterprise management, entrepreneurial teams, enterprise structure, HRM aspects, staffing, and enterprise culture
- Technological management—aspects of current technology for operational management
- Legislation-related issues—legal aspects and taxation aspects
- Innovation—*innovation* aspects

What is a business plan?

A *business plan* is a formal document containing the goal(s) of a business venture, start-up, or small and medium-sized enterprise

(SME); the methods of attaining those goal(s); and the time frame for the achievement of the goal(s). It also describes the nature of the business, background information on the business, financial projections, and the plan it intends to implement to achieve the stated targets. In other words, a business plan is a written summary of an entrepreneur's proposed business venture, start-up, or SME; its operational and financial details; its marketing opportunities and strategy; and its entrepreneurial management skills and abilities.

The business plan serves two essential functions. It guides the enterprise's operations by charting its future course and devising a strategy for following it. It furnishes a battery of tools: a mission statement, objectives, budgets, financial forecasts, target markets, and strategies to help entrepreneurial management lead the enterprise successfully. It gives entrepreneurial management and employees of business venture, start-ups, and SMEs a sense of direction.

The second function of the business plan is to attract investors or lenders. The best way to attract investors without a solid business plan rarely attracts needed capital. It should demonstrate that the entrepreneur of a business venture, start-up, or SME has thought seriously about the enterprise and what will make it succeed. The entrepreneur of a business venture, start-up, or SME is the driving force behind the business idea and is the one who can best convey the vision and the enthusiasm he/she has for transforming that idea into a successful enterprise. There is no substitute for a well-prepared business plan, and there are no shortcuts to creating one.

In brief, the business plan serves as an entrepreneur's road map on the journey toward building a successful business venture, start-up, or SME. The business plan allows you to gain control over your business venture, start-up, or SME and enables you to promote a competitive advantage over industry rivals. In brief, it describes the basics of your business venture's, start-up's, or SME's operations and forecasts. The format should be easy to read, understand, and change. The business plan brings together all aspects of the business venture, start-up, or SME, including the product/service, market, and strategy. As mentioned above, it serves as a road map that provides direction to the business the entrepreneur undertakes.

It describes every aspect of a particular business venture; it includes a marketing plan, clarifies and outlines financial needs, identifies potential obstacles and has alternative solutions, establishes milestones for continuous and timely evaluation, and serves as a communication tool for all financial and professional sources. In other words, a *business plan* is the major tool used in guiding the formation of the business venture as well as the primary document in managing it. It is more than a written document. It is a process that starts when entrepreneurs begin to gather information and then continues as projections are made, implemented, measured, and updated. In other words, it is an *ongoing process.*

The business plan helps the business venture, start-up, or small and medium-sized enterprise (SME) individuals to determine the viability of their venture and convince others to provide financing. It describes the venture and its future, provides financial projections, and includes plans for marketing, manufacturing, and other business functions. The plan should describe at length the people involved in the enterprise and a full assessment of the opportunity including consumers/customers they serve and competitors they encounter, the environmental context including regulatory and economic perspectives, and the risk they face including future risks and how the venture owners intend to deal with them.

Students of entrepreneurship education are taught to see the formulation of their potential business venture ideas. In business plan courses, the students describe and define their business, provide a description of their management team and business organizational structure and description of the market, decide on their marketing plan and business system, and select an implementation of the business idea with respect to finance, risk, and cash flow. In other words, it is also a program that prepares students/individuals to undertake the formation and operation of their business venture, start-up, or small and medium-sized enterprise (SME) for the purpose of performing all business functions relating to a product/service with emphasis given to social responsibility, legal requirements, and risks for the sake of profit involved in the conduct of a private enterprise. Entrepreneurship education should include a comprehensive overview of the competencies needed to be a successful entrepreneur as well as specialized knowledge in areas of particular need.

The programs would include the following:

- Understanding the nature of small business venture
- Determining your potential as an entrepreneur
- Developing the business plan
- Obtaining technical assistance
- Choosing the right type of ownership
- Planning the marketing strategy
- Locating the business location
- Financing the business venture
- Dealing with legal issues
- Complying with government regulations
- Managing the business venture
- Managing human resources
- Promoting the business venture
- Managing sales efforts
- Keeping the business records
- Managing the finances
- Customer relations management

Below is the *outline* of a *business plan*:

- Title page—A business plan has a title; and it contains the name of the business venture, start-up, or SME (small and medium-sized enterprise).
- Table of contents—It lists the name of each section and the page number where the section begins and their subheadings.
- Executive summary—This identifies the key areas you want to emphasize. Summarize the highlights including the identification of unmet consumer/customer needs, strategic fit, strategic and financial aspects, risk and major assumptions, and the initial recommendations. In short,

summarize all sections briefly as this should be just a page or two in length.

- The business venture, start-up, or SME vision statement—This touches everyone associated with the enterprise (employees, investors, lenders, consumers/customers, and the community in the market landscape). It is an expression of what the enterprise stands for and believes in. It is based on values.

- Mission statement—A mission statement expresses in words the entrepreneur envisions for his/her enterprise and what it is to become. It is the broadest expression of an enterprise's purpose and defines the direction in which it will move. It essentially sets the tone for the entire enterprise.

- Background of business venture, start-up, or SME

- Product/service and industry

- Description of product(s)/service(s)—The entrepreneur should describe the enterprise's overall product(s)/service(s), giving an overview of how consumers/customers use its product(s)/service(s).

- The market—This is a description of the market segmentation, trends in the market landscape, and consumers'/customers' needs and competitors' comparison.

- Market and target audience (customers/consumers)

- Overall strategy—A more important part of the business plan is the entrepreneur's view of the strategy needed to meet and beat the competitors. It should explain how the entrepreneur plans to gain competitive edge in the market. In this section, formulate a technological strategy with the current digital technologies.

- Marketing plan—This describes how to get the products/services to the targeted market of consumers/customers.

- Competitive analysis—In this section the competitors to the business venture, start-up, or SME are evaluated, including the market share, level of commitment, strengths, weakness, trends, and potential threats. Identify your competitors, their products/services, and their operations. Competitive analysis is an ongoing process and continues while the business venture, start-up, or SME exists. Most of the business ventures, start-ups, or SMEs gather information about competitors and the external business environment informally.

It is vital to know and understand the competition and keep track of the activities of competitors. This information is systematically and ethically collected from public sources and effective interviewing skills. Competitive analysis uses competitive intelligence to make good business plans and decision making or strategy. An entrepreneur has got to do competitive analysis as a part of the process when he/she begins in making the business plan. Identify competitors and try to differentiate your products/services from your direct competitors, their operations, etc. Try to do SWOT analysis: their *strengths*, *weakness*, *opportunities*, and *threats*. This is a marketing/management tool to evaluate a company's competitive position.

- Growth research and development plan
- Business venture, start-up, or SME legal and structure of the company
- Key personnel
- Related service providers
- Location of the business venture, start-up, or SME
- Financial plan
- Critical risks involved
- Income statement
- Cash flow projection
- Balance sheet
- Business venture, start-up, SME costs
- Schedule

The positive effects of entrepreneurship education are that it helps a country's economic growth, creates jobs, increases social resilience, promotes individual growth, increases engagement of schools/colleges/universities, and also improves equality. For the past several decades, there is worldwide exponential growth in entrepreneurship education in almost all institutions. The primary reason is that entrepreneurship education enriches entrepreneurship and entrepreneurial management as a major engine for economic growth and job creation in every country in the world.

Entrepreneurship education should focus on developing *innovation*, risk taking, imagination, and problem-solving skills or decision-making skills. As mentioned earlier, these skills can be developed through relevant course/programs. In short, students of entrepreneurship education should be presented with open-ended situations that require them to work through problems and situations with changing conditions. Through this process, students of entrepreneurship education will develop skills of adapting to new information and making decisions with imperfect knowledge. Entrepreneurship education should mainly be practically oriented and not be overloaded with theoretical expositions.

Investing in entrepreneurship around the world is considered as one of the higher return of investments (ROI). Entrepreneurship education can equip students with an entrepreneurial mindset. Acquiring know-how of entrepreneurship would lead individuals (he/she) to take ownership of their business ventures, start-ups, or SMEs. In brief, they acquire entrepreneurial skills such as communication, teamwork, critical thinking, problem solving, and risk taking.

The strong economic growth and job creation has propelled entrepreneurship education to a prominent position in higher education level. There are many opportunities with entrepreneurship education, such as its capacity to trigger deep learning and instill engagement, joy, motivation, confidence, and feelings of relevancy among college/university students. It also has some effects on job creation, economic success, and *innovation* for individuals, organizations, and society at large.

Entrepreneurship education is now being taught in colleges and universities in almost all countries. In twenty-first century in Western countries, we find students are showing an interest in business venture creation and independent employment and are seriously considering entrepreneurship as career option. Even throughout the globe, students who are interested in entrepreneurship as a career choice is growing. In the European Union, entrepreneurship education has spread considerably over the past several years.

Although entrepreneurship education is flourishing, numerous questions have to be clarified, such as the number of programs/courses, publications by lecturers/professors, impacts on the community, business venture creation by students and young graduates, and the resulting *innovation*. The role of entrepreneurship in economic progress is critical to the dynamics of a society and its future well-being. In business schools, courses/programs of entrepreneurship education are usually taught by lecturers/professors who are primarily educated in management, marketing, accounting, finance, and economics. This leads to a strong emphasis on management theories as the fundamental theoretical background in entrepreneurship education.

The courses/programs of entrepreneurship education have got to be designed and developed to introduce to the students the principles of business and management. This would tend to teach students how to become proficient and successful entrepreneurs. The entrepreneurship students would also learn about the entrepreneurial process; opportunity recognition; entry strategies; market opportunities and marketing; creating a successful business plan; financial projections; venture capital; debt and other forms of financing; external assistance for business venture, start-up, and small business enterprise; legal and tax issues; intellectual property; franchising; and entrepreneurship economics. It is so important that students of entrepreneurship education understand such principles and practices, especially if they are to go on to create their own business ventures.

Although entrepreneurship education is flourishing around the globe, numerous complex questions have to be clarified. An example is the question of evaluating entrepreneurship education program. This includes the number of courses/programs to be offered in colleges/universities, impacts on the community, business venture creation by students of entrepreneurship education, publications by teachers/lecturers/professors, and the results of *innovation*. Colleges/universities have got to promote entrepreneurial activities in partnership with their students and the business community with the objective of encouraging self-employment as career path as well as, to the young people, the basic competency skills and knowledge required for the creation of new business ventures, start-ups, and SMEs. Colleges/universities have got to offer a wide range of entrepreneurship awareness and educational activities.

In most of the developed countries—especially in Australia, countries in Western Europe, and US—the evaluation of entrepreneurship education program is attracting a lot of interest from academics and researchers. There is a development seen in numerous colleges/universities offering entrepreneurship courses. Globally several studies indicate that there is an increase in the supply of university-level courses/programs, such as new business venture foundation, business plans, small business venture management, and project management. In the past several decades, there has been a progressive increase in courses/programs, incubators, and other entrepreneurial activities oriented toward promoting entrepreneurship in developed countries.

In countries like Sweden, Finland, United States, Australia, Japan, United Kingdom, France, Belgium, Netherlands, Denmark, Italy, and Germany, entrepreneurship education has been recognized as an important subject area in many institutions. It is included as part of their curricula with the expectation that this could help to promote entrepreneurship. The main focus of such courses/programs is to teach entrepreneurship students what entrepreneurship is about, how to be entrepreneurial, the qualities of an entrepreneur, and what type of environment encourages entrepreneurship. As a matter of fact, these courses are designed and developed to meet increasing demands of young individuals who wish to pursue livelihoods requiring entrepreneurial skills.

In developed countries, formal education is considered to be a key factor in developing entrepreneurial skills of potential entrepreneurs. In formal education, entrepreneurship education primarily focuses on structured course materials that are designed and developed to prepare students to be able to identify, understand, and be aware of the entrepreneurial skills that can be applied in real-life circumstances.

Many programs/courses in entrepreneurship education focus on commonly identified entrepreneurial management and business-planning skills. But colleges and universities ignore entrepreneurial skills such as *innovation* and risk taking. In entrepreneurship education, entrepreneurial skills tend to be technical with insufficient attention paid to the cognition and belief systems of the entrepreneur. Teaching/lecturing in colleges and universities should take into account entrepreneurial attitudes and perceptions when designing and developing their entrepreneurship education and program/course objectives.

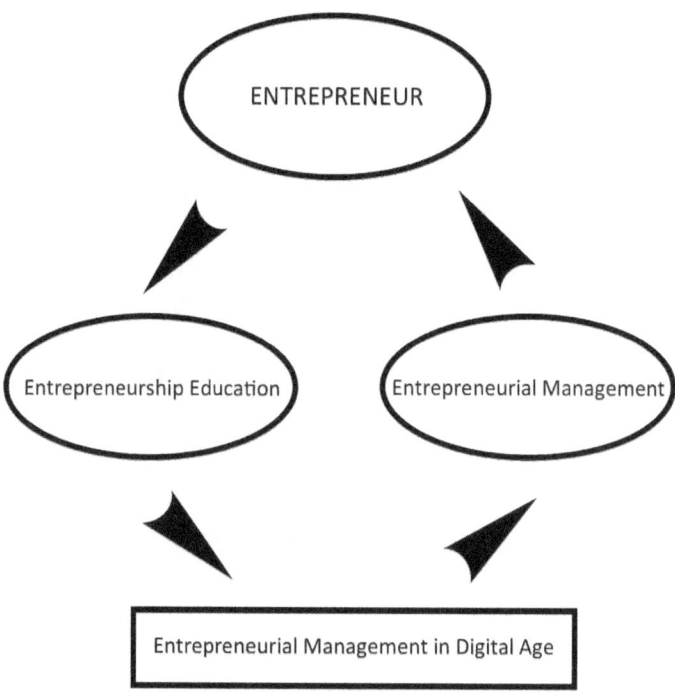

Fig: 3 The Entrepreneur's Management Education Life Cycle

CHAPTER 5

ENTREPRENEURSHIP EDUCATION IN COLLEGES/UNIVERSITIES AROUND THE WORLD

Entrepreneurship education programs/courses are gaining prominence around the world. In some of the universities, entrepreneurship education is increasingly introduced as a compulsory subject. Nowadays colleges/universities are offering both international business and entrepreneurship education courses/programs preferably in an integrated format. Therefore, international business is exciting to students, and the demand for international business education is skyrocketing in most of the universities in the Western Hemisphere. Investing in entrepreneurship education around the globe is considered as one of the highest return of investments, rather called as *return of investment* (ROI). Students of entrepreneurship education can equip themselves with an entrepreneurial mindset.

Acquiring know-how of entrepreneurship would lead the individuals (he/she) to take ownership of their business venture. In short, they acquire entrepreneurial skills such as teamwork, communication, problem-solving skills, critical thinking, and risk taking. The positive effects of entrepreneurship education are that it helps a country's economic growth, creates jobs, increases social resilience, promotes individual growth, increases engagement of colleges/universities, and also improves equality among citizens. Over a decade ago, there is a worldwide exponential growth in almost all institutions. The primary reason is that entrepreneurship as a major engine for economic growth and job creation has propelled entrepreneurship education to a prominent position in higher education level. There are many opportunities with entrepreneurship education such as its capacity to trigger deep learning and instill engagement, joy, motivation, confidence, and feelings of relevancy among college/university students. It also has some effects on job creation, economic success, innovation for individuals, organizations, and society at large.

Most of the entrepreneurship education courses focus on commonly identified entrepreneurial management and planning skills but ignore entrepreneurial skills such as *innovation* and risk taking. The teaching of entrepreneurial skills tends to be technical, with insufficient attention paid to the perception and belief systems of the entrepreneur. Lecturer/professors should take into account entrepreneurial attitude and perceptions when designing and assessing their entrepreneurship education programs and coursse objectives. Since entrepreneurship is a dynamic process, entrepreneurship education needs to focus on developing *innovation*, risk taking, imagination, problem solving, and decision-making skills.

Entrepreneurship education has been widely adopted by colleges and universities in many continents of the world. We see the rise of the service economy, the baby boom, and the growth of start-ups in the Western world. Colleges and universities around the world should promote entrepreneurial activities in partnership with their students and business community with the aim of *encouraging self-employment* as a career path as well as giving young individuals (he/she) the basic competencies, skills, and know-how required for the creation of new business ventures.

Another aspect of entrepreneurship education is social background of students. It plays a crucial role in their attitude toward becoming entrepreneurs. Labor market structure around the world is currently changing. Completing college/university no longer guarantees a job, and young individuals have got to face the uncertainty and complexities of the labor market. However, colleges/universities can play a role in helping to reduce unemployment by developing entrepreneurs. In other words, entrepreneurship education can be a way to legitimize entrepreneurship and develop an entrepreneurial culture with the purpose of fostering economic growth, developing and stimulating entrepreneurial skills, and preparing students for a dynamic labor market of a country.

Since it is possible to correctly identify those young male/female students possessing entrepreneurial potential, entrepreneurship education should be extended as broadly as possible throughout the total educational curriculum to catch in its net all those who might later fulfill the role of entrepreneur.

Global List of Colleges/Universities Offering Entrepreneurship Education

United States

- University of Arizona McGuire Center for Entrepreneurship offers undergraduate as well as graduate courses. Eller School of Entrepreneurship Education holds several programs/courses in entrepreneurship education including *innovation, research,* and *business plan.*
- Babson College offers undergraduate and graduate courses. They conduct dozens of undergraduate courses/programs and research related to entrepreneurship education.
- Ball State University Entrepreneurship Center offers undergraduate as well as graduate courses.
- Baylor University's John F. Baugh Center for Entrepreneurship conducts undergraduate and graduate courses. They have scholarships from private enterprises.

- Brigham Young University Rollins Center for Entrepreneurship offers undergraduate and graduate courses.
- California State University in Hayward conducts undergraduate as well as graduate courses/programs.
- University of California Haas Business School offers undergraduate and graduate courses.
- Carnegie Mellon University Swartz Center of Entrepreneurship offers undergraduate as well as graduate courses. They conduct continuing entrepreneurship education courses.
- University of Colorado Boulder Deming Center for Entrepreneurship offers undergraduate and graduate courses. They have several scholarships.
- Columbia University offers undergraduate and graduate studies.
- Cornell University offers undergraduate and graduate courses.
- DePaul University conducts undergraduate and graduate courses. They have an MBA program for entrepreneurship.
- University of Georgia offers undergraduate and graduate courses.
- Harvard University offers undergraduate as well as graduate courses.
- University of Illinois Chicago offers undergraduate and graduate courses. They hold an MBA program concentrated in entrepreneurship.
- University of Iowa Tippie College of Business conducts undergraduate and graduate courses. They conduct more than two dozens of undergraduate and graduate courses/ programs and certificate courses in entrepreneurship education.
- Kennesaw State University's Michael A. Leven School of Management and Entrepreneurship offers undergraduate and graduate courses.

- University of Louisville Forcht Center for Entrepreneurship offers undergraduate as well as graduate courses. They teach more than a dozen of courses/programs in entrepreneurship education.
- University of Maryland conducts undergraduate and graduate courses.
- University of Nebraska offers undergraduate and graduate courses.
- New York University offers undergraduate and graduate courses. They conduct a dozen of graduate courses/programs in entrepreneurship education.
- Northwestern University Farley Center conducts undergraduate as well as graduate courses.
- Ohio State University offers undergraduate and graduate studies
- Oklahoma State University School of Entrepreneurship offers undergraduate and graduate courses.
- University of Pennsylvania offers undergraduate and graduate courses.
- St. Louis University Chaifety Center for Entrepreneurship offers undergraduate as well as graduate courses.
- University of St. Thomas offers undergraduate and graduate courses. They hold more than a dozen of graduate and undergraduate courses/programs in entrepreneurship education.
- San Diego State University Lavin Center offers undergraduate and graduate courses.
- Syracuse University offers undergraduate and graduate courses.
- Thunderbird University offers undergraduate and graduate courses.
- University of Southern California Lloyd Greif Center offers undergraduate and graduate courses.
- Syracuse University offers undergraduate and graduate studies

- University of Texas at Austin Entrepreneurship at McCombs conducts undergraduate and graduate courses.
- University of Wisconsin–Madison Weinert Center for Entrepreneurship offers undergraduate as well as graduate courses.
- Xavier University offers undergraduate and graduate courses. They conduct more than two dozen undergraduate and graduate courses/programs in entrepreneurship education.

Canada

- Acadia University
- University of British Columbia
- St. Francis Xavier University
- Ryerson University
- University of Saskatchewan
- University of Toronto
- Bishop's University
- Queen's University
- The University of Waterloo
- University of Western Ontario
- Wilfrid Laurier University

Mexico

- Technológico de Monterrey

Argentina

- San Andres University

United Kingdom

- Royal Holloway, University of London
- University of Strathclyde, Scotland

- University of Edinburgh Business School, Scotland
- University of Cambridge
- Imperial College, London
- University of Birmingham
- Lancaster University
- University of Oxford
- London Business School
- University College London
- University of Brighton
- Nottingham Trent University
- Sheffield Hallam University
- University of the West of England, Bristol
- Cardiff University
- University of Leicester
- Manchester Metropolitan University
- Teesside University, Middlesbrough
- Durham University
- Swansea University
- University of Warwick
- London School of Economics

European Union

- University of Amsterdam
- Utrecht University
- Ghent University, Belgium
- HEC Paris Business School
- Grenoble Ecole de Management
- IESE Business School
- ESMT Berlin
- University of Leipzig
- University of Passau
- Hamburg University of Technology
- University of Florence
- EU Business School
- University of Southern Denmark

- Copenhagen School of Entrepreneurship

Norway

- The Norwegian School of Entrepreneurship

Sweden

- Halmstad University
- Linnaeus University
- KTH Royal Institute of Technology
- Jonkoping University
- University of Gothenburg

Australia

- University of Melbourne
- Queensland University of Technology
- University of Technology Sydney
- Swinburne University of Technology
- Western Sydney University

New Zealand

- The University of Auckland
- University of Otago
- Massey University

Asia

- National University of Singapore
- Nanyang Technological University
- Seoul National University
- Yonsei University
- Korea University
- Bengkulu University

- Universiti Teknologi Mara, Malaysia

India

- Indian Institute of Technology
- Chandigarh University
- NMIMS University
- NITU University

Indonesia

- Petra Christian University
- Benghulu University

Middle East

- Mansourna University, Egypt
- Helwan University, Egypt
- Ain Shams University, Egypt
- University of Jerusalem, Israel
- Hebrew University of Jerusalem TAU's Collier School of Management
- Tel Aviv University, Israel

South America

- Ibmec, Rio De Janeiro, Brazil

In developed countries such as Britain, United States, France, Germany, and Japan, some lecturers/professors in universities are turning themselves into successful entrepreneurs by developing innovative ideas and by facilitating the transfer of technological breakthrough from universities to industry. Over two decades ago, the University of Strathclyde in Scotland, UK, offered courses in entrepreneurship education known as Entrepreneurship Initiatives, which was comprised of an *innovation* class, an interactive computer-based class. An introduction to entrepreneurship course/program was introduced with the involvement of academics, alumni, and entrepreneurs.

Through the Entrepreneurship Initiatives, students in any year or any department at the university were able to take an entrepreneurship class, earning credit toward their degree. In later years, the classes were designed to maximize the benefits students gain from participating in open-ended classes, entrepreneurs in classes, guest presenters, group projects, video case studies, multimedia, computer-aided learning, workshops, and webinars. The Entrepreneurship Initiatives teamed up with specialists to develop their classes and associated learning materials etc.

Entrepreneurship education classes include the following:

- Entrepreneurship—business start-up tool kit (multimedia)
- Introduction to entrepreneurship
- Entrepreneurship to personal creativity
- Entrepreneurship to new venture creation
- Entrepreneurship to knowledge-, science-, and technology-based business

Entrepreneurship education was designed and developed in one of the universities in Europe. The program at University of Ghent in Belgium enhanced the intellectual, managerial, entrepreneurial, and personal development of graduate students in order to improve their capacity to plan, start up, and manage new business ventures. The goals of their entrepreneurship education are in a broad range, varying from the acquirement of specific knowledge on the start-up and management aspects of new business ventures and the identification and simulation of entrepreneurial skills to the creation of an awareness of the process involved in the initiation and management of a company. The university has undergraduate and graduate levels of entrepreneurship education.

The following courses/programs are taught in the undergraduate level:

- Introduction of management (contents include searching for and implementing ideas and developing a business plan)
- Financial management (contents include venture capital)
- Marketing (contents include market focus)
- Industrial management (contents include development of a business plan)

The following courses/programs are taught in the graduate level:

- Financial management (contents include venture capital)
- Human resources management (contents include problems and solutions within a business)
- Financing (contents include venture capital and growth financing)
- Tax management (contents include fiscal aspects of start-ups and growth)

Besides undergraduate and graduate levels of education at the university, the school also offers courses in introduction to entrepreneurship and business economics. The learning methods include lectures, assigned readings, workshops, writing business plans, class discussions, webinars, case studies, etc. The writing of business plan plays an important part in teaching entrepreneurship. They combine business plan with field project in which the students are supposed to write a business plan for new business ventures.

CHAPTER 6

ENTREPRENEURIAL MANAGEMENT

The major functions of management are generally accepted to be planning, organizing, leading, and controlling. The four functions are continuous and interrelated. Planning begins the process as the entrepreneurial management determines what to do. Organizing involves assembling the resources such as the financial and human resources and materials needed to accomplish the plan. Leading is the process of getting the most output possible from those resources. Controlling is comparing what the management initially planned with what was actually accomplished.

Entrepreneurial management is a technique of management that is proactive, opportunity driven, and action oriented. It involves strategic decisions and operating management philosophies. Entrepreneurial management is a unique style of managing that requires coping with challenges and difficulties they encounter in different phases of the development of enterprises. Entrepreneurial managers have got to possess specific competencies to successfully perform the challenging tasks and roles of the management in their business ventures, start-ups, or SMEs. They also have to concentrate on leadership competencies that the entrepreneurial management needs to develop in different phases of their enterprises, growth, and development.

The following are important skills that an entrepreneurial manager must have to plan, organize, lead, and control:

- Develop relationships with peers
- Carry out negotiations
- Motivate employees
- Resolve conflicts
- Establish information networks
- Make decisions in allocating resources efficiently and effectively
- Willing to learn continually

It is widely known that businesses, start-ups, and SMEs can be an important engine of *innovation* in industrialized economies. An entrepreneurial manager usually tries to establish and balance the *innovation* abilities of the business with the efficient and effective use of resources available. Innovativeness of an entrepreneurial manager is characterized by their ability and tendency to think creatively, develop cutting-edge ideas in opportunity recognition, and utilize resources and their problem-solving skills. Entrepreneurial management skills include leadership and management, developing entrepreneurial management systems and techniques, and team building in business ventures, start-ups, and SMEs. Entrepreneurial managers in business ventures, start-ups and SMEs have got to learn from their work environment so that they could acquire the relevant knowledge, skills, and competencies necessary for the long-term survival and success of the enterprises they manage.

Entrepreneurial management incorporates the knowledge and skills believed to be essential for implementing and sustaining a business venture, start-up, or a small and medium-sized enterprise (SME). In brief, entrepreneurial management utilizes the know-how of entrepreneurship to increase the effectiveness of a new business venture, start-up, or small and medium-sized enterprise (SME) by human resources management, operations management, logistics management, marketing management, accounting management and finance management, and also Internet technologies management.

Entrepreneurial management philosophy incorporates organizational process and structures to promote agility, flexibility, creativity, and continuous *innovation*. Entrepreneurial management is a discipline of leadership framework. It is not a replacement for traditional management. In other words, it is a discipline designed to help leaders become as rigorous in the entrepreneurial part of their management portfolio as they are in the general management part. It requires different tools and different safeguards from the ones we are accustomed in traditional management settings.

As entrepreneurship is also a team sport, entrepreneurial managers have to deal with lots of different people daily, all of whom present social barriers to overcome, whether it's geography, culture, or language. Entrepreneurial managers have got to understand people well enough to get them to overcome their barriers and deliver their best effort. Entrepreneurial managers pull together capital, resources, and technology to create new business ventures and to revitalize existing businesses. The task is to take these components and add value to them, thereby providing new products/services.

Entrepreneurship starts with ideas and transforms them into realities. Entrepreneurs are forces of energy, change, creativity, and dynamism. Entrepreneurial management is concerned with new ideas, directions, relationships, concepts, methods, and modes of operation. Special attention is given to business plans that create competitive advantages. In short, entrepreneurship is the single most important factor in stimulating the creation of jobs and encouraging competitiveness and economic growth. Setting up an entrepreneurial tone and establishing an innovative value system in the new business venture, start-up, or small and medium-sized enterprise (SM) are critical factors of successful entrepreneurial management. In other words, innovative spirit is an essential part to respond to new market needs in the market landscape.

Entrepreneurial management is the practice of taking the know-how in entrepreneurship to increase the effectiveness and efficiencies of new business ventures. In order to be successful in a business venture, start-up, or small and medium-sized enterprise (SME), it is necessary to do more than creating a new product or services; an entrepreneur has to have managers who can create an operating system that will let a new business venture, start-up, or small and medium-sized enterprise (SME) survive and prosper. A key characteristic of a good entrepreneurial management is to have fundamental management principles by which they organize the business venture.

Those entrepreneurs that manage to grow their business venture are likely to go through different stages or business venture types. These are individual venture, team business venture, hierarchy, and complex hierarchy. In the latter two types, the organizing starts to resemble that of large enterprises, and the activities are often closer to managerial ones rather than entrepreneurial. For a new business venture, start-up, or small and medium-sized enterprise (SME) entrepreneur, it is advisable to keep salary costs down; and this can be done not only by using subcontractors but also paying on individual actions and outcomes.

In management perspective, entrepreneurial management is a management system under which members of the business venture, start-up, or small and medium-sized enterprise (SME) are empowered to think and act like employees. All employees of a business venture, start-up, or small and medium-sized enterprise (SME) keep the overarching goals as well as the benchmark objectives of the entire venture, start-up, or small and medium-sized enterprise (SME) in mind. Employees are also empowered to build their autonomy and accountability by engaging in decision making that involves calculated risks and by taking responsibility for those outcomes.

Management education is an effective way of providing business ventures with the management expertise they require. When it comes to traditional management and entrepreneurial management, entrepreneurial management controls and deploys (for example, finance) resources to create an innovative economic business venture for the purpose of profit on growth under the condition of risk and uncertainty whereas traditional management get things done through and with individuals (marketing, human resources, accounting, and operations) in a company or group of companies. In other words, management is an individual person or group of individuals that accept responsibilities to run the company or group of companies to achieve the objective of the company or group of companies. The management skills of an entrepreneur indicate how well he or she can perform vital activities in a business venture.

The following management skills are considered as successful factors for an entrepreneur:

- A well-thought-out new business venture, start-up, or small and medium-sized enterprise (SME) plan ensures that the entrepreneur can establish the business venture confidently. In short, it is necessary to research and plan.
- To have management skills and use advisers/experts when necessary
- Customer service, combined with good public relations, ensures that an entrepreneur is sensitive to the customers' needs.
- Successful entrepreneurs know who their competitors are, how many there are and how influential they are, what each one's share of the target market is, and what the quality of their products/services are like.
- Be market oriented.
- Realize the importance of quality products/services.
- Accounting/bookkeeping for personal purposes
- Insight into costs, income, profit, and loss
- Successful entrepreneurs exercise financial disciplines and understand how money should be spent and what it should be spent to ensure success.

Entrepreneurial management involves setting clear objectives, creating opportunities, empowering employees, preserving organizational intimacy, and developing human resources systems. Entrepreneurial management is also the ability to influence others and to manage resources strategically. Entrepreneurial management has gone to involve idea generation, idea structuring, and idea promotion, where idea generation is important in the initial stage of a business venture, start-up, or SME and idea structuring and promotion in the latter stage.

Entrepreneurial management entails influencing and directing the performance of employees of a business venture, start-up, or SME toward the achievement of the enterprise's objectives.

Entrepreneurial management incorporates the knowledge and skills believed to be essential for both implementing and sustaining a business venture, start-up, or small and medium-sized enterprise (SME). Entrepreneurs concerned need to be able to recognize opportunity—for example, those resources, transactions, and collaborations with the potential for improving the existing situation.

Entrepreneurs should also know how to classify these potential opportunities appropriately, make inferences in regard to consequences, design procedures for implementation, and coordinate the activities of various individuals and groups required to enact the opportunity. In short, the entrepreneurial management of the business venture, start-up, or SME must be able to design a system capable of achieving and sustaining multiple goals through the recognition and innovative utilization of all available resources. The fundamental problems encountered in entrepreneurship—such as how to discover opportunities, how to evaluate the attractiveness of industries, how to get resources, and how to create competitive advantage—may be explained by more general economic and management theories such as *network, consumer behavior*, and *transactions cost.*

At most colleges/universities, entrepreneurship education is usually conducted by lecturers/professors who are well versed in economics and management. This leads to a strong emphasis on management theories as the fundamental theoretical background in entrepreneurship education. The organization of a business or a business venture is the collection of individuals who work together and coordinate their actions to achieve a wide variety of objectives; and the management of a business venture, start-up, or small and medium-sized enterprise (SME) is the individuals responsible for supervising and making the most of a business venture's human resources to achieve its objectives/goals. So entrepreneurial management is the planning, organizing, leading, delegating, and controlling of humans and other resources to achieve objectives/goals of a business venture, start-up, or small and medium-sized enterprise (SME) efficiently and effectively.

The resources of a business venture, start-up, or SME include assets such as people and their skills, know-how, and experience; machinery; raw materials; computers and information technology; financial capital; and customers and employees. In the entrepreneurial management's perspective, the following courses/programs can be taught at colleges/university levels: introduction to management and business plan, financial management, marketing, human resources management, and financing and tax management.

The writing of a business plan is an important method in teaching the principles of entrepreneurship. The writing of a business plan is often combined with a field project in which the students of entrepreneurship have to write a business plan for a real new business venture. Inside the lecture/classroom, there are some classical tools which can be utilized for entrepreneurship education such as lectures, case studies, readings, workbook exercises, and writing papers. There could be class discussions, discussion with experts and guest speakers, individual coaching, role plays, team teaching, and teamwork.

Entrepreneurial management skills in a nutshell

- Plan the new business venture, start-up, or small and medium-sized enterprise (SME) before establishing it. Entrepreneurs usually plan informally because they do not have time to draft a formal business plan and/or simply they do not know how to do it. It is a vital part of opening a new business venture since it has the following advantages: Fewer mistakes will be made because problems can be identified in the planning stage, so the entrepreneur will therefore be wiser as a result of the planning. Entrepreneurs are obliged to address all important factors of the planned business venture and will therefore depend less on purely instinctive and crisis decisions. This prevents stress and future-oriented action. The planning stage is an ideal opportunity for testing ideas. Business planning process is an entrepreneurial management function. It takes a narrow view of the business venture's infrastructure. It gives guidance concerning how to link and execute the functional activities to achieve maximum investment turnover. The linking principles are smooth and synchronized process flows, investment turnover and increase in profits, excess of waste in resources, quality costs, etc.

- Have entrepreneurial management skills and use advisers and/or experts when necessary. Entrepreneurs usually know what their strengths and/or weaknesses are in respect of the business venture they are operating or intend to operate. They do have to utilize their management skills and personal characteristics effectively. In order to compensate, entrepreneurs have got to use consultants, contractors, or professional experts and/or advisers.

- Customer service, combined with good human relations, ensures that an entrepreneur is sensitive to the clients' needs. Personal service is vital for entrepreneurs. Technical and/or administrative factors are also important for good customer service.

- Knowledge of competitors are important. Each one's market share of the target market and quality of their products have got to be in the entrepreneur's radar. Entrepreneurs have got to investigate competitors' strengths and/or weaknesses.

- Successful entrepreneurs are market oriented. They know who their target market is, what the target market's requirements are and their needs, and how to meet these needs profitably.

- Realize the importance of quality products/services. To do this, costs must be kept under control without affecting the quality of the products. Quality products and services contribute to the marketing of the business ventures because they ensure new customers through personal recommendations of existing satisfied customers.

- Entrepreneurs have got to understand their accounting/bookkeeping systems for decision making to better manage their business ventures, start-ups, or small and medium-sized enterprises (SMEs).
- Entrepreneurs have got to know which costs are essential for survival and understand the implications of increased expenditure.
- Successful entrepreneurs exercise financial disciplines and understand how money should be spent and what it should be spent on to ensure success. They must constantly make decisions on expenses to be incurred. They have to develop the ability to make the right decisions for ensuring growth.

CHAPTER 7

ENTREPRENEURIAL MANAGEMENT IN DIGITAL AGE

We currently live in the digital age. Digital technologies have profoundly transformed the ways we do business, work, and live. In other words, it offers new ways of connecting, collaborating, conducting enterprises, and building bridges among entrepreneurs and consumers/customers. In brief, digital technology's transformation can improve productivity, improve profitability, boost speed in the delivery of products/services, and leverage consumer/customer satisfaction into loyalty. Every business venture, start-up, and SME is seeking to improve its productivity. To achieve improved productivity, business ventures, start-ups, and SMEs have got to implement *innovation* that can help employees collaborate, communicate, and work better. For example, cloud computing feature allows users/employees to access files regardless of where they are. This allows employees to work wherever and whenever there are consumers/customers, vastly improving productivity and collaboration.

*How do digital technologies help in transforming the
experience of consumers/customers in business
ventures, start-ups, and SMEs, which in turn facilitate
the entrepreneurial management in digital age?*

Transforming the consumers'/customers' experience is at the
heart of digital transformation. In other words, digital technologies
are transforming the game of consumers'/customers' interactions
with new rules and possibilities that were unthinkable. In brief, the
digital technologies are tools that can be amalgamated to get closer to
consumers/customers in the market landscape. If business ventures,
start-ups, and SMEs utilize these tools appropriately, an engaging
consumer/customer experience creates value for both consumers/
customers and enterprises. It drives retention and stimulates loyalty
of consumers/customers. Digitally engaged consumers/customers
expect that products/services and information will be timely and well
suited to their specific needs. Consumers/customers want to have
all these at the explicit moment they are looking and on whatever
platform they are using at the time. The more touch points business
ventures, start-ups, and SMEs have, the greater the complexity of the
interactions across channels and the greater the need to understand
consumers/customers in detail. Therefore, business ventures, start-
ups, and SMEs need to thoroughly understand both consumers'/
customers' behaviors and the enterprises' requirements to deliver the
new consumer/customer experience.

Business ventures, start-ups, and SMEs have got to understand
that digital transformation cannot happen without investment in
digital technologies. But smart investment in digital technologies can
creatively enhance consumer/customer experience. Business ventures,
start-ups, and SMEs must be aware that the size of the investment is
not important but the impact is. To business ventures, start-ups, and
SMEs, new digital technologies such as social media, mobile technology, and analytics are only tools to get closer to their consumers/
customers in their market landscape. For business ventures, start-
ups, and SMEs, consumer/customer data play an important role as
these data are the lifeblood for designing compelling consumer/cus-

tomer experience. So entrepreneurial management will have access to precious data that can substantially increase their insights in the consumer/customer experience. Business ventures and SMEs will also have the ability to integrate these data to make better decisions, increase the quality of the personalized experience, and create true competitive advantage.

Furthermore, digital technologies create many opportunities for business ventures, start-ups, and SMEs to orchestrate supply-chain management better. For example, merchandise suppliers, service providers, or even consumers/customers can share information on a real-time basis. Digital technologies are fostering a more transparent sharing of information up and down but also across the enterprise. Zoom meetings, video communications, and webcasts are allowing employees of business ventures, start-ups, and SMEs from all functions, regardless of their location, to come together to solve problems or innovate.

For more than two decades, there is an enormous increase in the use of advanced technologies in business ventures, start-ups, and SMEs. Through advanced technologies, business ventures, start-ups, and SMEs are contributing more to a country's economy. Cutting-edge-technology has made it easy in processing day-to-day business activities and routine tasks. The tech wave has been building for a long time but has accelerated in recent years. The past decade has witnessed an enormous progress in digital technologies. In the digital age, the enterprise's ability to communicate with consumers/customers effectively and moreover the enterprise's growth capability are determined on how their employees can effectively interact and sell their products/services. Transforming the consumer/customer experience is at the heart of digital technologies. In other words, digital technologies are transforming the game of consumer/customer interactions with new rules and possibilities that were unimaginable a decade ago.

Digitally engaged consumers/customers expect that products/services and information will be timely and tailored to their specific needs. These consumers/customers need all of these products/services at the precise moment they are seeking them and on whatever platform they are utilizing at the time. Business ventures, start-ups, and SMEs have got to thoroughly understand both consumer/customer behaviors and the enterprise requirements to deliver the new consumer/customer experience. Business ventures, start-ups, and SMEs must bear in mind that transformation of digital technologies cannot happen without digital investment.

In the twenty-first century, entrepreneurship has revealed itself as one of the vital forces in the global digital economy and in the study of entrepreneurial management in the digital age. In the digital age, the digital workplaces of business ventures, start-ups, and SMEs are comprised of employees working under entrepreneurial managers where workplaces are all about the employees' ability to do their jobs by collaborating, communicating, and connecting with others. Their objective is to plod along productive business relationships within and beyond work groups and to enable sharing of knowledge across the business. The integration of digital technology into everyday life and the process of making everything digital is known as digitalization. It creates new opportunities for *innovation* and growth.

There are opportunities for entrepreneurial managers such as

- improving the entrepreneurial manager's decision making, particularly in social media technologies and Internet of Things (IoT) as better decision making helps to improve performance in sales/marketing;
- enhancing interactions among consumers/customers, suppliers, and employees; and
- enabling customer/consumer service.

Digital transformation is the process of utilizing digital technologies to create new or modify existing business processes or culture and customer/consumer experiences to meet changing businesses in digital age. In brief, the process of utilizing digitized information, making established ways of working simpler and more efficient manner, is known as digitalization.

Digital technology, Internet, and mobile technologies have transformed the way business ventures, start-ups, and SMEs operate. So there are numerous business ventures, start-ups, and SMEs around the globe that have not implemented the cutting-edge technology as yet. In digital age, they have got to implement Internet and mobile technologies in their planning process. Digital technologies can fuel *innovation* and improve performance of the business venture, start-up, or SME but only if applied in the right places and with the right amount of investment. Mobile/smartphone technologies furnish remote and transient collaboration and communication capabilities by enabling anytime and anywhere voice, data, and services access.

These technologies encompass software applications and various types of supporting networks. There are advantages/benefits by having digital technology. They can utilize digital technology to reduce business costs and improve customer relationships. There is an enterprise software available for them to automate office functions such as record keeping, accounting, and payroll. Smartphones / mobile phones allow their home office and field representatives to interact in real time. Business ventures, start-ups, and SMEs can utilize technology to create a secure environment for maintaining sensitive business and consumer/customer information.

Many of the entrepreneurial management bodies are convinced that the success of business ventures, start-up, and SMEs in twentieth century's hypercompetitive environment depends upon creativity, *innovation*, flexibility, and agility. The creativity, *innovation*, and entrepreneurship are interrelated. The creativity is having a new idea whereas innovation is doing something with that idea such as creating a product/service. In other words, creativity can lead to *innovation* when it comes to entrepreneurship, and it's more of a process.

Digital technologies are the endless agitators of the enterprise world. The pace and impact of digital technologies have been nothing short of astonishing, but they are just a prelude for what's to come. Digital technology has contributed to several changes in the entrepreneurial management. Digital technology has changed the way people live and the way they communicate and work. Creating great consumer/customer experiences or market-leading operational capabilities is more than a technology challenge. The usage of digital technology can boost profitability of a business venture, start-up, or SME, as well as the speed of entering a product/service market landscape, and also improve customer/consumer expectations.

In the digital age, business ventures, start-ups, and SMEs have greater options for effective communications to increase their productivity rates and to save costs by automating their operations under entrepreneurial management. The entire entrepreneurial management can utilize computer systems, which include desk/laptop computers, smartphones, software and applications, high speed Internet, and IoT for transporting their operations with an intention to compete with competitors in their market landscape.

In the digital age, business ventures, start-ups, and SMEs can easily access business software and databases to add or gather details. Employees can utilize their smartphone / mobile devices to complete various business-related tasks. Using these devices, employees of business ventures, start-ups, and SMEs can accomplish their assignments/tasks in real time, which can eventually increase their productivity and revenues of the business. In brief, entrepreneurial management can utilize different software and apps to automate their operations and processes, such as a computerized maintenance management system to automate maintenance management.

Digital technology has transformed the way entrepreneurial management works in chasing the goals/objectives of the business venture, start-up, or SME. Virtual meetings and videos conferences via Zoom and Skype are increasingly implemented by business ventures, start-ups, and SMEs to keep their operations running. Digital technology in business ventures, start-ups, and SMEs helps to solve cost reduction, return on investment (ROI), and also the ability to turn transparency into agility. In other words, digital technology in business ventures, start-ups, and SMEs offers both enterprise and personal benefits such as saving money and redeploying resources.

Moreover, digital technology eliminates waste. Entrepreneurial management can have better operations strategy as well as better decision making. Entrepreneurial management in digital age has become more business oriented with the aim of assisting and interacting with supervisors and others in the business ventures and decision makers to gain understanding of the financial impacts of decisions and taking on a proactive business-oriented role. Digital technology has enabled the level of analysis of products/services and pricing to become more refined and frequently updated.

The Internet technology is considered as a strategic resource where business ventures, start-ups, and small and medium-sized enterprises (SMEs) can promote their products/services into new territories within a country. This is the primary reason why business ventures, start-ups, and small and medium-sized enterprises (SMEs), which are in enormous competition, are oriented toward the market fulfilling the requirements of the consumers/customers. These business ventures, start-ups, and small and medium-sized enterprises (SME) can utilize Internet technologies strategically to gain a competitive edge in lowering costs, *innovation*, promotion of growth, improving quality and efficiency, also increasing consistency, etc. In other words, Internet technologies can transform the way business ventures, start-ups, and small and medium-sized enterprises (SMEs) compete.

Once SMEs move past their start-up stage, they encounter the setting up of day-to-day operations that can support growing business demands. Internet and mobile/smartphone technologies provide remote and transient collaboration and communication capabilities by enabling anytime and anywhere voice, data, and services access. Mobile/smartphone technologies encompass software applications, various categories of supporting networks, and corresponding hardware. Many business ventures, start-ups, and SMEs exploit mobile/smartphone applications for new business opportunities, better consumer/customer reach, smoother interaction with their own employees, and operational growth.

Employees of business ventures, start-ups, and SMEs are now expected to work in virtual teams and be always available to interact at any point in time. In short, mobile/smartphone technologies enables workers of business ventures, start-ups, and SMEs to remotely access resources to complete their work tasks, extending their connectivity and reach. The entrepreneurial management has to consider security challenges posed by using mobile/smartphone technologies. In order to addresses this issue, entrepreneurial management needs to identify security protocol and shape employee behaviors that may limit their traditional flexibility.

Business ventures, start-ups, and SMEs have got to limit sensitive data downloads on mobile/smartphones, which could be subject to theft / loss.

In today's digital age, *proper mix of internet technologies* can furnish a competitive advantage for a business venture, start-up, or SME. Gaining a competitive advantage through the use of Internet technologies is the proper fit. Therefore, multiple Internet technologies are needed by the business venture, start-up, or SME.

From a consumer/customer service perspective, *broadband computing* plays a vital role for a business venture, start-up, or SME. Again, from the consumers'/customers' perspective, broadband provides significant bandwidth, which allows for impressive speeds in the delivery of information. Furthermore, it increases the network speed. It also provides significant cost savings while offering improved support. With broadband computing, business ventures, start-ups, and SMEs would be able to work effectively with satellite workspaces. They can have multiple workers and no central office. Broadband computing furnishes additional flexibility for workers by allowing them to work from home.

As this technology and connectivity continue to expand, the acceptance of business ventures, start-ups, and SMEs of remote work is increasing; and majority of decision makers are more accepting of working off-site. Working from home furnishes the benefit of work-life balance to the workers, and having the ability to work from home provides workers the ability to fulfill personal activities during the normal working hours with minimal interruption to work responsibilities. In short, the flexibility of remote work impacts productivity. Job satisfaction is also positively impacted by remote work. Broadband computing expands reach, allowing business ventures, start-ups, and SMEs to access consumers/customers and resources previously unavailable. These enterprises with larger aspirations now have a greater chance of reaching their previously out-of-reach consumers/customers and resources through broadband technologies.

These enterprises also have the ability to serve a much wider range of consumers/customers.

Digital technology, in entrepreneurial management perspective, helps the business venture, start-up, or small and medium-sized enterprise (SME) to achieve integration, to minimize costs of communication, to enhance efficiency, and to increase sharing of information, which will lead to improved performance. In today's digital age, it is virtually impossible for business ventures, start-ups, and SMEs to function without a web presence. They can utilize the Internet to gather information about their industry and competitors and exchange emails to facilitate networking with customers/consumers and suppliers.

Cloud computing and *virtualization* have triggered the creation of another Internet technology specialization—cloud computing management. Cloud computing can play an important role in using web-based software. Business ventures, start-ups, and SMEs can facilitate communication among suppliers and consumers/customers. Cloud computing has become an integrated part of digital technology. They can connect to available physical or virtual environments, utilizing different entry points for that matter. They, too, can access information online in a twenty-four-seven basis from a desktop, laptop, or smartphone. For business ventures, start-ups, and SMEs, cloud computing makes it cheaper with low costs and flexibility at workplace. It also improves data security and allows them to shorten the delivery time. The cost of having software applications such as customer relation management (CRM), enterprise resource planning (ERP), project management (PM), sales, marketing, accounting applications on their premises/offices is so enormous. So it is more cost effective to have these software applications in the cloud.

Inventory management is a significant for business ventures, start-ups, and SMEs and can create severe strain on cash flow. Cash flow determines how much inventory can safely be carried by a business venture, start-up, or SME while still allowing sufficient cash for other operations. Cash flow is the difference between the amount of cash actually brought into the enterprise and the actual amount paid out in a given period of time. Cash flow represents the lifeblood of a business venture, start-up, or SME.

The inventory turnover ratio lends insight to this situation. Usually inventory represents the largest capital investment for most of business ventures, start-ups, and SMEs. Surplus inventory yields a zero rate of return and unnecessarily ties up the enterprise's cash. In other words, the cost of carrying inventory is expensive. Even carrying too much inventory increases the chances that the enterprise will run out of cash. Cloud computing in Internet technologies helps enormously in inventory management of a business venture, start-up, and small and medium-sized enterprise (SM) to store and access data instead of in a hard drive of a computer. There are subscription-based cloud computing services available for business ventures, start-ups, and small and medium-sized enterprises (SMEs). Even big data represents human-generated data from a variety of sources such as social media, transactions, emails, and so forth. Internet of Things (IOT) helps inventory management operations like warehousing, shipping, and retail outlets for business ventures, start-ups, and small and medium-sized enterprises (SMEs).

Business ventures, start-ups, and SMEs need to have accurate financial information to know the financial health of the enterprise. To make effective entrepreneurial management decisions, enterprises must know things like how much the accounts receivable are worth, how old each account is, how quickly inventory is turning over, which items are not moving, how much the enterprise owes, when the debts are due, and how much the enterprise owes in taxes etc. Therefore, the accounting function is critical in the successful operation of business ventures, start-ups, and SMEs. The function furnishes the entrepreneurial management with relevant information for planning, decision making, and control. The decision-making functions of an entrepreneurial management in a business venture, start-up, or SME affect the entire enterprise. As a result, it is often difficult to specify the types of decision-making information needed by the entrepreneurial management.

In the digital age, business ventures, start-ups, and SMEs are finding that success or failure is increasingly dependent on their entrepreneurial management and the utilization of information. The accountancy management has changed dramatically over the past years with Internet technologies. With the advent of numerous software and advanced accounting software, the entrepreneurial management that deals with accounting function in business ventures, start-ups, and small and medium-sized enterprises (SMEs) has changed a great deal for the past four decades. Nowadays the entrepreneurial management that deals with the accounting function makes use of the Internet technologies to coordinate services to streamline the accounting functions. They utilize cloud computing to reduce Information technology expenses, which are "savings" that can be passed on to customers of business ventures, start-ups, and small and medium-sized enterprises (SMEs).

The two most popular accounting software for business ventures, start-ups, and SMEs are *FreshBooks* and *QuickBooks*.

FreshBooks

It has a well-designed interface with lots of features such as tracking payments. It can be used even by someone who is not familiar with accounting. It also allows you to set up an automatic payment reminder. It saves time by creating recurring invoices. There is an advanced payments feature which provides more secure and faster payment processing provided by WePay and Stripe. There is an expense creation screen where you can add vendors, select the cost of goods, and mark the expense as billable within seconds. FreshBooks can be accessed via a cloud-based web application and smartphone application. This makes it easy for business ventures, start-ups, and SMEs to log in, check important statistics, log expenses, and generate invoices instantly. It also integrates with many applications such as SalesForce, Shopify, PayPal, Zapier, Stripe, Capsule, Revamp, CRM, Agile CRM, Hurdlr, Acuvity, Basecamp, Asana, GSuite, and HubSpot.

QuickBooks

It can track income and expenses, invoices, and tax deductions; accept payments; run reports; capture and organize receipts; send estimates; track sales and sales tax; and track miles and features a payroll service. It also features bill management and time tracking and can track projects and inventory and manage contactors. It offers a desktop version, the cloud-based QuickBooks platform. QuickBooks can be integrated with many applications and platforms such as transactions from PayPal, Square, and banks and financial institutions and can be linked to Shopify and other e-commerce platforms to track sales and sales tax, process payments with mobile credit card readers or POS, and file payment of taxes. Download the QuickBooks applications on both Android and iPhones and link with Bill.com to automate your accounts payable process. Sync Method:CRM to keep track of all customer interactions.

The advent of Internet technologies has contributed enormously to the change in the way that the human resource management accomplishes their tasks in business ventures, start-ups, and small and medium-sized enterprises (SMEs). Human resource management plays an important role in business ventures, start-ups, and small and medium-sized enterprises (SMEs). The human resources management controls day-to-day operations such as hiring, developing, and managing employees and maintaining protocols and procedures; so they become an important asset in business ventures, start-ups, and small and medium-sized enterprises (SMEs). Internet technologies play a vital role in in recruiting via online. This allows a business venture, start-up, or small and medium-sized enterprise (SME) to easily control the recruitment process from a computer. Online recruiting reaches a larger audience from a wide geographical area. The other benefits are the low cost and the efficient and direct communication between human resource management and job seekers.

We are currently living in the digital age where information plays a vital role in our daily lives. Information systems are important in this age for their role in gathering, processing, storing, transforming, and distributing information for planning, decision making, and control of business ventures, start-ups, and SMEs. In this digital age, enterprises are finding that success or failure is increasingly dependent upon their entrepreneurial management and use of information.

Entrepreneurs believe that it is the know-how that the entrepreneurial management needs to understand and utilize current advanced technologies and to know how accounting information systems gather and transform data into useful decision-making information for business ventures, start-ups, and SMEs in the digital age.

Besides FreshBooks and QuickBooks, there is artificial intelligence in accounting such as the ES (expert system), which is useful in financial and management accounting, income taxes, and auditing. Most of the accounting applications are computerized. The areas of accounting where expert systems are usually applied are cash management, accounts receivable, accounts payable, expenses, inventory, payroll, plant and equipment, etc. Accounting systems within a business venture, start-up, or SME is an ideal area for expert system applications.

When it comes to accounting applications, expert systems are ideal for cash flows, accounts receivable, and accounts payable for business ventures, start-ups, and SMEs. In short, expert system is designed to solve specific problems such as how to reduce cost and improve productivity and quality for business ventures, start-ups, and SMEs. Expert systems can be used for accounting, auditing, competitive analysis, financial analysis, manufacturing and capacity planning, resources planning, scheduling, strategic planning, marketing, etc.

Four areas of accounting in which expert system are particularly useful are

- accounting standards,
- taxation,
- entrepreneurial management control, and
- auditing.

Expert systems can also be utilized for

- maintaining ledgers,
- preparing financial statements,
- planning budgets and forecasts,

- preparing and analyzing payroll,
- analyzing expenses, and
- reviewing all financial aspects of the business venture, start-up, or SME.

Expert systems even work well for financial applications such as granting of credits, insurance claims processing, etc. for business ventures, start-ups, and SMEs.

An expert system, sometimes referred to as knowledge system, is a set of computer programs that perform a task at the level of a human expert. In terms of artificial intelligence, expert systems are created on the basis of knowledge gathered on specific topics from human experts, and they imitate the reasoning process of a human being. Entrepreneurial management can utilize expert systems to solve specific problems, such as how to reduce costs (example, production costs) and improve employee productivity.

Expert systems have two databases, namely subject database and knowledge database. The subject database contains all the facts about a particular subject. This set of data is similar to an enterprise's database—for example, an enterprise's financial status of the enterprise. The knowledge database contains procedural rules that dictate which actions to follow. Rule-based expert systems process knowledge in a structured format and work well for accounting applications where entrepreneurial management can easily make decisions with the use of questionnaires.

Expert systems offer the following advantages/benefits for business ventures, start-ups, and SMEs:

- They increase output/productivity.
- They offer better accuracy, quality, and reliability.
- They enhance problem-solving capabilities.
- They improve the decision-making process.
- They improve consumer/customer service.
- They are capable of training novices or new employees.
- They are easy to modify by adding and deleting rules.

BambooHR

BambooHR software offers tools to handle every aspect of human resource management. It is exclusively for SMEs. It offers employee data and attendance, new hires, onboarding, compensations, and work culture. It features employee information on positions/titles, salary, and benefits. Administrators can track time-off requests, set accrual policies and holidays, and generate different types of reports. Administrators can create job openings and post them on job boards such as Indeed and Glassdoor. Employees can edit personal information, request time off, and access company documents and general information. It provides an add-on that allows account managers to export payroll data from BambooHR and process it through TRAXPayroll or another payroll-specified software.

JazzHR

JazzHR software offers business ventures, start-ups, and SMEs a simple dashboard to keep track of their recruiting/hiring process. It gives human resource managers the ability to customize recruiting workflow, research candidates, and perform background checks. It tracks upcoming interviews and job openings. It links with Indeed, LinkedIn, Glassdoor and Monster.com.

In the twenty-first century, business ventures, start-ups, and SMEs are able to operate globally because of access to state-of-the-art communications system technology and to data and information made widely available through low-cost technology; and this access clearly makes doing business across globally more affordable for SMEs. SMEs usually participating only in domestic economy now face competition and find opportunity outside their boundaries. As an entrepreneur, his/her role is to create new business ventures, implement new technologies, and stimulate growth and wealth in the economy.

The following are the characteristics of a successful entrepreneurial manager:

- Personal skills
- Thinking style—in other words, creating a shared vision of a realistic, credible, and attractive future for the betterment of the new business venture, start-up, or SME.
- Operating on resources
- Foresight—how the vision fits the business venture
- Hindsight—does not violate policies, tradition, and culture and with a competitive view
- Depth perception—has appropriate responses from competitors and understands responses from competitors
- Communication abilities
- Persistence
- Trust
- Ability to keep up to date and keep learning
- Interpersonal skills—builds coalition between people and information sources and has the top-level management support
- Understands the process of innovation and change for the business venture

Guidelines for a new business venture, start-up, or small and medium-sized enterprise (SME):

- Be a leader, not a follower. In your new business venture or start-up, you are part of the *executive* team. You do have to show the team why you believe *innovation* will drive the success of a new business venture or a start-up.
- Culture plays a play a vital role to your success. It includes team work, collaboration, and honesty.
- *Innovation* requires a committed level of resources such as people, money, time, and equipment. Business ventures, start-ups, and SMEs are increasingly encountered with intensifying competitive pressures. Consumers/customers

pose an even more stringent demands regarding unique-
ness, customization, speed of delivery, quality of products/
services, etc. In order to ensure their competitiveness, business ventures, start-ups, and SMEs have got to meet these
challenges by furnishing a continuous stream of new and
improved products/services.

- You do have to set the *vision* in order for the leadership to
outline an *innovation* agenda.

Twenty-first century is the era of entrepreneurship. It does create new jobs. It also creates new opportunities to improve the structure or better the quality of products/services as well as the quality
of life of every country's economic growth. Many countries around
the globe have launched initiatives to boost entrepreneurship. Digital
technology not only is a driving force for a country's economic
growth and business ventures but also assists like a powerful force in
shaping the entrepreneurs' behavior, nature, and mindsets. Digital
technology can help drive business venture success. But it requires
that engagement in the business venture to understand the potential of current technology. Entrepreneurial management has to think
broadly about enabling change rather than relying on traditional
functions of information technology.

In the digital age, technology and data transform every step of
the business venture process. All employees of a business venture,
start-up, or SME under entrepreneurial management have a responsibility to keep abreast with the latest cutting-edge digital technology
impacting their role in the business venture, start-up, or SME. This
can reap tremendous benefits for the business venture, start-up, or
SME as staying up to date on digital tools means staying ahead of the
competitors of yours. The innovation of digital technology brings
with it a wave of fresh start-ups and new business ventures. In short,
Internet technologies can help to drive the success of a business venture, start-up, or SME. But it requires the entrepreneurial management in the business venture to understand the potential of current
technology. Entrepreneurial management has to think broadly about
enabling change rather than relying on traditional functions of infor-

mation technology. In the digital age, technology and data transformation transform every step of the business process.

In the entrepreneurial management's perspective, digital technology can improve customer/consumer service by offering outstanding services to all customers/consumers, allowing them to interact with the business venture, start-up, or SME throughout the years. In brief, utilizing web-based self-service applications, customers/consumers can receive personalized products/services each time they visit the business venture, start-up, or SME. In other words, when all systems integrated, the business venture, start-up, or SME will always be equipped with accurate, timely information necessary to quickly respond to customer/consumer needs and queries.

When business ventures, start-ups, and SMEs have integrated systems, they will deliver products/services faster and cheaper. Customers/consumers of the business venture, start-up, or SME become satisfied and share their satisfaction to other potential customers/consumers. As business ventures, start-ups, and SMEs operate with integrated technology, they lower their operating costs as well as the quality of the products/services. Business ventures, start-ups, and SMEs work online with suppliers to facilitate inventory management that provide products/services faster and cheaper. In short, a business venture, start-up, or SME becomes more efficient with integrated technologies.

As part of integrated technologies within a business venture, start-up, or SME, employees, customer/consumers, and suppliers can perform transactions by utilizing web-based self-service application. The self-service aspect eliminates intermediaries and delays, significantly reduces administrative errors, accelerates billing and accounting procedures, lowers communication costs, and helps deliver important documents. Digital technology in business ventures, start-ups, and SMEs helps business intelligence to make accurate, timely decisions and gives them the ability to monitor its impact across the business venture, start-up, or SME.

Artificial intelligence will create new roles and transform the role of the entrepreneurial management. When it comes to entrepreneurial management in the digital age, AI (artificial intelligence) plays a crucial role in the years to come. AI, as it is more commonly called, has become more prominent in conversations about technology these days among marketing management and marketing research professionals and entrepreneurs around the globe. But what does artificial intelligence mean? How might it shape the future of entrepreneurial management?

In many ways, artificial intelligence is already at work in market/marketing research and in market field surveys. But entrepreneurial management are excited about its potential power to process big data and learn from it at a pace that far outstretches the capability of human capacity. Artificial intelligence can automate repetitive tasks and sort data. It is proficient at providing deep insights into consumers and optimizing workflow. The potential of artificial intelligence is that it has the capacity to recognize patterns, trends, and insights of the consumers' minds. In other words, artificial intelligence can detect buying patterns of consumers.

It also identifies insights and highlights valuable relationships that human may miss. It drives customer demands and expectations higher, forcing entrepreneurs to deliver better experiences. Entrepreneurs will learn new technical skills to get ahead. Artificial intelligence makes selling tasks more efficient by enhancing data-driven decision making. Entrepreneurs will be able to identify their target consumers and understand the customers' needs better.

The computing power of artificial intelligence has increased exponentially for the past several years. It holds tremendous potential in the analytics of small and big data. In many ways, artificial intelligence is the key to unlocking the power of massive amounts of data in the market landscape. Among all different artificial intelligence applications, ES (expert systems) are the most promising for business ventures, start-ups, and SMEs. The applications include problem solving, planning, and monitoring. It also covers accounting, finance, management, and marketing.

Entrepreneurial managers have not experienced the full potential of artificial intelligence (AI). Artificial intelligence is proficient at providing deep insights into consumers and optimizing workflow.

It will create new roles and transform the role of entrepreneurial management.

Artificial intelligence makes selling tasks more efficient by enhancing data-driven decision making. Artificial intelligence drives consumer/customer demands and expectations higher, forcing entrepreneurs to deliver better experiences. It provides social insights that allow entrepreneurs to deliver message across various channels based upon consumer/customer behavior. Artificial intelligence will always need the entrepreneurs' input to maximize its value. Entrepreneurial management will learn new technical skills to get ahead.

Digital technologies are reaching into every corner of the enterprise world, bringing deep transformations in how business ventures, start-ups, and SMEs are structured and led and how they perform and compete with others. The author feels confident that other technologies will be even more transformational. The history of technological progress—particularly, the progress with digital technologies—is one of constant surprise. The world abounds with ever more potential *innovators* and entrepreneurs, and they have got to access to more and more increasingly powerful computing technologies all the time at lower costs.

Artificial intelligence is transforming the global digital economy. Several small, medium, and large enterprises have seen high growth by implementing artificial intelligence in their enterprises through automation and leveraging data analytics in digital age. Artificial intelligence-powered customer relations management (CRM) enables business ventures, start-ups, and SMEs to identify serious buyers and build stronger connections with consumers/customers by tapping into data from past interactions and similar leads.

Artificial intelligence and customer relations management (CRM) let business ventures, start-ups, and SMEs analyze the enormous amount of consumer/customer data available across social channels in real time. Business ventures, start-ups, and SMEs can also gain deeper understanding of their consumers/customers and on how they perceive their products/services with AI-based CRM.

AI helps business ventures, start-ups, and SMEs grow and transform the field of entrepreneurial management, particularly in the decision-making process. These enterprises save time and effort by automating their business processes and enable their employees to work productively in a digital economy. It will help business ventures, start-ups, and SMEs achieve their business objectives and create strong competitive advantages. AI helps in consumer/customer care, reduces energy costs, also helps enterprises to be more consumer—or customercentric, performs data analysis, and ensures cybersecurity defense.

When it comes to consumer/customer service, AI has a chatbot tool that imitates human conversation with users over websites, mobile applications, telephone, etc.—in other words, artificial intelligence-powered digital assistants that communicate with consumers/customers in the market landscape. It improves consumer/customer service and boosts consumer/customer engagement. AI analyzes communications with consumers/customers and generates highly targeted offers for the consumers/customers. It also showcases the products/services of the business venture, start-up, or SME. Thus, it brings new leads and increases revenues. Artificial intelligence-powered sentiment analysis can help business ventures, start-ups, and SMEs understand consumers/customers and gain insights to improve products/services. It also boosts consumer/customer service.

Artificial intelligence automates repetitive tasks, which can help business ventures, start-ups, and SMEs achieve greater output in less time at lower cost. In brief, AI can improve the speed of business operations. As enterprises grow, the risk of cybersecurity exponentially increases, such as identity thefts, account takeovers, etc. Artificial intelligence-powered cybersecurity allows business ventures, start-ups, and SMEs detect abnormal behavior that causes damages to the enterprise.

When it comes to competitive intelligence, AI can track everything that competitors of a business venture, start-up, or SMEs do, from products/services to consumer/customer service. Artificial intelligence-powered competitive research can help business ventures, start-ups, and SMEs capture information about their competitors' every move, expose threats, and discover what consumers/customers are telling about their competitors and their products/services. AI is for every enterprise that aims to grow and stay ahead of their competitors.

Artificial intelligence presents business ventures, start-ups, and SMEs with a wide variety of unique benefits and opportunities. In short, AI can empower business ventures, start-ups, and SMEs to furnish better, more relevant experiences to their consumers/customers and forge bonds with them.

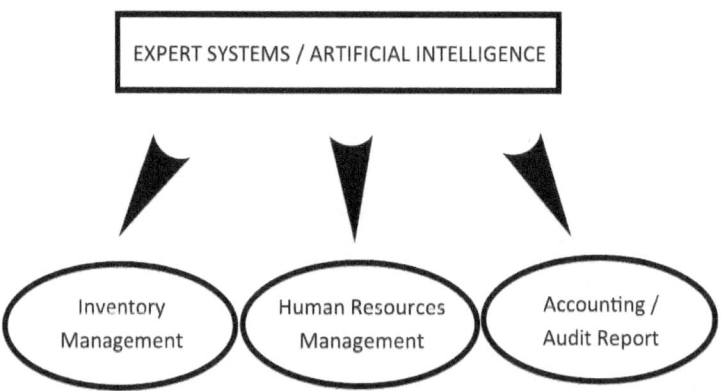

Schematic diagram: EXPERT SYSTEMS / ARTIFICIAL INTELLIGENCE
ease ENTREPRENEURIAL MANAGEMENT

GLOSSARY

Accounting. It is a system that provides quantitative information about the finances of a business entity or an individual. It includes recording, measuring, and describing financial information.

Accounts payable. It is a list of debts currently owed by a business or a person. These are debts incurred mainly for the purchase of services, inventory, and supplies. The accounts normally do not include accrued salaries payable, accrued interest payable, or rent payable.

Accounts receivable. It is a list of money owed on current accounts to a creditor, which is kept in the normal course of the creditor's business and represents unsettled claims and transactions. Accounts receivable normally arise from the sale of an enterprise's products/services to its customers.

Access method. A protocol that controls which device accesses the shared network medium and the way a device accesses the network.

Accounting. A system that provides quantitative information about the finances of an enterprise entity/an individual. Includes recording, measuring, and describing financial information.

Accounts payable. List of debts currently owed by an enterprise or a person. These are debts incurred mainly for the purchase of services, inventory, and supplies. The accounts normally do not include accrued salaries payable, accrued interest payable, or rent payable.

Accounts receivable. List of money owed on current accounts to a creditor, which is kept in the normal course of the creditor's business and represents unsettled claims and transactions. Accounts receivable normally arise from the sales of an enterprise's products/services to its customer.

Address. With respect to networks, a unique code that identifies a node in the network.

Application. A software program specifically designed for a particular task or the specific use of a software program.

Application programming interface. A set of calling conventions defining the interface to a service.

Architecture. The specific components of a computer system and the way they interact with one another.

Artificial Intelligence (AI). Branch of computing that deals with using computers to simulate human thinking. Artificial Intelligence is concerned with building computer programs that can solve problems creatively, rather than simply working through the steps of a solution designed by a programmer.

Assets. Every business has assets, which is its simplest terms are items with value. All businesses need assets to produce/sell services. An asset is anything a business owns.

Balance sheet. Financial statement that gives an accounting picture of property owned by a company and of claims against the property on a specific date. The left (debit) side of a balance sheet states assets; the right (credit) side shows liabilities and owner's equity. The two sides must be equal (balance). The balance sheet is like a snapshot of the position of an individual or business at one point in time.

Budget. Estimate of revenue and expenditure for a specific period. Of the many kinds of budgets, a cash budget shows cash flow, an expense budget shows projected expenditures, and a capital budget shows anticipated capital outlays. The term refers to a preliminary financial plan. In a balanced budget, revenue equal expenditures.

Business plan. A document designed to detail the major characteristics of a business—its product/service, its industry, its market, its manner of operating [production, marketing, management], and its financial outcomes on the business's present and future.

Business venture. Business venture is a new business that is formed with a plan and expectation that financial gain will follow.

Cash flow. The actual receipt and spending of cash by a business.

Competitive advantage. The particular way a business implements consumer/customer benefits that keeps the business ahead of other businesses in the market landscape.

Consumer. Ultimate user of a product/service. The consumer is not always the purchase of a product/service. Consumers are considered to be users of the final product/service.

Creativity. A process producing an idea or opportunity that is novel and useful, frequently derived from making connections among distinct ideas or opportunities.

Customer relations management (CRM). The process of tracking the customer's different contacts with the business, and utilizing this data to help improve revenues as well as the customer's experience.

Customer service. Function of a company that responds to inquiries/complaints from customers of that company. It is an important part of the fulfillment function, ensuring that customers will buy again and/or continue to be good customers.

Entrepreneur. Individual who initiates business activity. The term is often associated with one who takes business risks.

Entrepreneurial management. Entrepreneurial management is the concept of utilizing the creative and innovative abilities, skills and expertise to efficiently open and manage a start-up business.

Entrepreneurship. Entrepreneurship is the creation/extraction of value. It is viewed as change, generally taking risk.

Equity. Equity is the value of the capital contributed by owners or stockholders.

Expert system. In computing Artificial Intelligence, a reasoning process that allows the computer to draw deductions, producing new information, modifying rules, or writing new rules. The computer is thereby allowed to learn from data it has stored.

Financial accounting. Accounting system that provides balance sheet and income statement results.

Fixed assets. Fixed assets are anything a business owns, such as buildings or equipment.

Innovation. Implementation of a creative idea or opportunity leading to profitable and effective outcomes.

Innovative strategy. An overall strategy approach in which a business seeks to do something that is very different from what others in the industry are doing.

Intellectual Property (IP). An intangible asset of value. The protection of IP—trademark, copyrights and patents—determine if you can prevent other people from copying these creations, and whether or not you yourself can use them freely.

Inventory control. Accounting system of maintaining inventories to prevent stock outs, reduce holding costs, and permit detecting theft.

Liabilities. Liabilities are amounts owned by a business at any one time. They can be expressed as payable for accounting purposes. Included in liabilities are loans, credit payments due, taxes, or any other form of debt in which you are obliged to pay.

Market research. Research conducted to uncover market and customer needs and opportunities; it exists at two levels, primary and secondary.

Marketing research. Systematic collection and interpretation of data to support future marketing decisions.

Marketing plan. Plan that details a company's marketing effort; also called action program, marketing strategy. The marketing plan may be laid out for an individual products/services.

Mission statement. Definition of a company's vision and values, often printed or plaques, posted on its website, and otherwise publicized. The mission statement typically emerges as part of the strategic planning process.

Profit and Loss statement. Profit and Loss statement is a business report that shows net income as the difference between revenue and expenses.

Return on investment (ROI). A capital budgeting equation used to measure the relationship between initial investment and the profits are expected to be received from making the investment.

Small medium enterprise (SME). Small medium enterprise is a business that maintains revenues, assets/number of employees below a certain threshold.

Start-up. A new business that is started from scratch. It is formed to develop a unique product/service, bring it to market landscape and make it irresistible and irreplaceable for consumers/customers.

BIBLIOGRAPHY

Abrahamson, Eric, and Gregory Fairchild. *Knowledge Industries and Idea Entrepreneurs: New Dimensions of Innovative Products, Services, and Organizations.* 2001.

Acs, Zoltan J., Thomas Åstebro, David Audretsch, and David T. Robinson. "Public Policy to Promote Entrepreneurship: A Call to Arms." *Small Business Economics* 47, no. 1 (2016): 35–51.

———, and Catherine Armington. "Employment Growth and Entrepreneurial Activity in Cities." *Regional Studies* 38, no. 9 (2004): 911–927.

———, and D. B. Audretsch. "Innovation and Technical Change." In *The International Handbook of Entrepreneurship*, 55–79. 2003.

———. "Innovation: Largely the Work of Small Firms." *Small Business Advocate* 15, no. 8 (1996): 11.

Ahmadi, H. H., and A. O'Cass. "The Role of Entrepreneurial Marketing in New Technology Ventures First Product Commercialization." *Journal of Strategic Marketing* 24, no. 1 (2016): 47–60.

Alberti, F. (1999). "Entrepreneurship Education Scope and Theory." In "Entrepreneurial Knowledge and Learning: Conceptual Advance and Directions for Future Research." *JIBS Research Report*, no. 6 (1999): 64–84.

Aldrich, Howard. E. "The Emergence of Entrepreneurship as an Academic Field: A Personal Essay on Institutional Entrepreneurship." *Research Policy* 41, no. 7 (2012): 1240–1248.

———. "Entrepreneurship." *Handbook of Economic Sociology*, (2005): 451–457.

Allen, Kathleen R. *Bringing New Technology to Markets*. New York: Prentice Hall, 2002.

Allinson, C. W., E. Chell, and J. Hayes. "Intuition and Entrepreneurial Behavior." *European Journal of Work and Organizational Psychology* 9, no. 1 (2000): 31–43.

Alvarez, Sharon A., and Lowell Busenitz. "The Entrepreneurship of Resource-Based Theory." *Journal of Management* 27, (2001): 755–775.

Anderson, B. S., J. Covin, and D. P. Slevin. "Understanding the Relationship between Entrepreneurial Orientation and Strategic Learning Capability: An Empirical Investigation." *Strategic Entrepreneurship Journal* 3, no. 6 (2009): 218–240.

Antonakis, J., and E. Autio. "Entrepreneurship and Leadership." In *The Psychology of Entrepreneurship*, 189–208. London: Routledge, 2007.

Ajzen, I. "Perceived Behavioral Control, Self-Efficacy, Locus of Control, and the Theory of Planned Behavior," *Journal of Applied Social Psychology* 32, (2002): 1–20.

Ardichvili, A., R. Cardozo, and S. Ray. "A Theory of Entrepreneurial Opportunity Identification and Development." *Journal of Business Venturing* 18, no. 1 (2003): 105–123.

Armstrong, P. *Critique of Entrepreneurship: People and Policy*. New York: Palgrave MacMillan, 2005.

Astebro, T., and I. Bernhardt. "Start-Up Financing, Owner Characteristics, and Survival," *Journal of Economics and Business* 55, no. 4 (2003): 303–319.

Atherton, A., and P. Hannon. "The Business Plan—a 21st-Century Dinosaur?" In *IntEnt95*, edited by H. Klandt and Muller-Boling. 1995.

Audretsch, David B., Alex Coad, and Agusti Segarra. "Firm Growth and Innovation." *Small Business Economics* 47, no. 1 (2014): 1–7.

————, I. Grilo, and A. R. Thurik. *Handbook of Research on Entrepreneurship Policy.* Cheltenham: Edward Elgar, 2007.

————, M. C. Keilbach, and E. E. Lehmann. *Entrepreneurship and Economic Growth.* Oxford University Press, 2006.

————, and M. Keilbach. "Entrepreneurship Capital and Economic Performance." *Regional Studies* 38, no. 8 (2004): 949–959.

Autio, Erkko, Martin Kenney, Philippe Mustart, Don Siegel, and Mike Wright. "Entrepreneurial Innovation: The Importance of Context." *Research Policy* 43, no. 7 (2014): 107–108.

————. "Growth of Technology-Based New Firms." *The Blackwell Handbook of Entrepreneurship,* (2000): 329–347.

Bagby, D. R., and P. Stetz. "Can Entrepreneurs Be Taught?" *The Art and Science of Entrepreneurship Education* 1, (1994): 23–31.

Bagheri, A., and Z. A. L. Pihie. "Entrepreneurial Leadership: Towards a Model for Learning and Development." *Human Resources Development International* 12, no. 4 (2011): 447–463.

Ballantine, J. W., and C. T. Koeller. "Characterizing Profitable and Unprofitable Strategies in Small and Large Businesses." *Journal of Small Business Management* 30, no. 2 (1992): 13–24.

Baron, R. A. "The Cognitive Perspective: A Valuable Tool for Answering Entrepreneurship's Basic 'Why' Questions." *Journal of Business Venturing* 19, no. 2 (2004): 221–239.

————. "Opportunity Recognition: How Entrepreneurs 'Connect the Dots' to Identify New Business Opportunities." *The Academy of Management Perspectives* 20, no. 1 (2006): 104–120.

————. "The role of Affect in the Entrepreneurial Process." *Academy of Management Journal* 33, no. 2 (2008): 328–340.

Baughn, C., and K. Neupert, K. "Culture and National Conditions Facilitating Entrepreneurial Start-Ups." *Journal of International Entrepreneurship* 1, no. 3 (2003): 313–330.

Baumol, W. J. *Entrepreneurship, Management, and the Structure of Payoffs.* Cambridge, Massachusetts: MIT Press / Macmillan, 1993.

————. "Entrepreneurship Productive, Unproductive, and Destructive." *Journal of Political Economy* 98, (1990): 893–921.

————. *The Microtheory of Innovative Entrepreneurship*. Princeton, New Jersey: Princeton University Press, 2010.

Bechard, J. P., and J.M. Toulouse. "Validation of a Didactic Model for the Analysis of Training Objectives in Entrepreneurship." *Journal of Business Venturing* 13, no. 4 (1998): 317–32.

————, and D. Gregoire. "Entrepreneurship Education Research Revisited: The Case of Higher Education." *Academy of Management Learning and Education* 4, no. 1 (2005): 22–43.

Bennett, R. J. *Entrepreneurship, Small Business and Public Policy*. London and New York: Routledge, 2014.

Benson G. L. "Thoughts of an Entrepreneurship Chair Holder Model Entrepreneurship Curriculum." *Journal of Applied Business Research* 9, no. 1 (1991): 140–146.

Berger, Brigitte. *The Culture of Entrepreneurship*. San Francisco: ICS Press, 1991.

Bergman, Thomas P., *The Essential Guide to Web Strategy for Entrepreneurs*. Upper Saddle River, New Jersey: Prentice Hall, 2001.

Bhide, A. V. "Bootstrap Finance: The Art of Start-Ups." *Harvard Business Review* 70, no. 6 (1992): 109–117.

————. "How Entrepreneurs Craft Strategies That Work," *Harvard Business Review* 72, (1994): 150–161.

Binks, M., and P. Vale. *Entrepreneurship and Economic Change*. London: McGraw Hill, 1990.

Bitler, M. P., T. J. Moskowitz, and A. Vissing-Jorgensen. "Testing Agency Theory with Entrepreneur Effort and Wealth." *Journal of Finance* 60, no. 2 (2005): 539–576.

Blanchflower, D. G., and A. J. Oswald. "What Makes an Entrepreneur?" *Journal of Labor Economics* 16, no. 1 (1998): 26–60.

Blackburn, R. A., and M. T. Schaper. *Government, SMEs and Entrepreneurship Development, Policy, Practice and Challenges*. Gower Publishing, 2012.

Block, Z., and S. A. Stumpf. *Entrepreneurship Education Research: Experience and Challenge the State of the Art of Entrepreneurship*. Boston, Massachusetts: PWS Kent, 1992.

Brand, M., L. Wakkee, and M. Van Der Veen. *Teaching Entrepreneurship to Nonbusiness Students: Insights from Two Dutch Universities.* 2007

Brazeal, D. V., and T. T. Herbert. "The Genesis of Entrepreneurship." *Entrepreneurship Theory and Practice* 23, no. 3 (1999): 29–45.

Brenner, O. C., C. C. Pringle, and J. H. Greenhaus. "Perceived Fulfillment of Organizational Employment versus Entrepreneurship: Work Values and Career Intentions of Business College Graduates." *Journal of Small Business Management* 29, no. 3 (1991): 62–74.

Brannback, M., and A. L. Carsrud. *Revisiting the Entrepreneurial Mind: Inside the Black Box.* Cham, Switzerland: Springer, 2017.

Brettel, M., and J. D. Rottenberger. "Examining the Link between Entrepreneurial Orientation and Learning Processes in Small and Medium-Sized Enterprises." *Journal of Small Business Management* 51, no. 4 (2013), 471–490.

Brocas, I., and J. D. Carillo. "Entrepreneurial Boldness and Excessive Investment," *Journal of Economics and Management Strategy* 13, (2004): 321–350.

Brockhaus, R. H. "Foreword." In *Entrepreneurship Education: A Global View*, edited by R. H. Brockhaus, G. E. Hills, H. Klandt, and H. P. Welsch. Aldershot: Ashgate, 2001.

———, and P. S. Horwitz. "The Psychology of the Entrepreneur." In *The Art and Science of Entrepreneurship*, edited by D. L. Sexton and R. W. Smilor. Cambridge: Ballinger, 1986.

Brophy, D. J. "Financing the Growth of Entrepreneurial Firms." In *Entrepreneurship 2000*, 5–27. Chicago, Illinois: Upstart Publishing, 1997.

Brown, R. "Encouraging Enterprise: Britain's Graduate Enterprise Program." *Journal of Small Business Management*, (October 1990): 71–77.

Buera, E. J. "A Dynamic Model of Entrepreneurship with Borrowing Constraints." *Annals of Finance* 5, (2009): 443–464.

Bull I., and G. E. Willard. "Towards a Theory of Entrepreneurship." *Journal of Business Venturing* 8, (1993): 183–195.

Burke, A., S. Fraser, and F. J. Greene. "Multiple Effects of Business Plans on New Ventures." *Journal of Management Studies* 47, no. 3 (2010): 391–415.

Busenitz, L. W., et al. "Entrepreneurship in Emergence: Past Trends and Future Directions," *Journal of Management* 29, no. 3 (2003): 285–308.

———. "Entrepreneurial Risk and Strategic Decision Making: It's a Matter of Perspective." *Journal of Applied Behavioral Science* 35, no. 3 (1999): 325–340.

Bygrave, W. D. "Theory Building in the Entrepreneurship Paradigm." *Journal of Business Venturing* 8, (1993): 255–280.

———, and C. W. Hofer. "Theorizing about Entrepreneurship." *Entrepreneurship: Theory and Practice* 16, no. 2 (1991): 13–22.

Camp, S. Michael. *The Innovation-Entrepreneurship NEUS: A National Assessment of Entrepreneurship and Regional Economic Growth and Development.* Powel, Ohio: Advance Research Technologies, LLC, Small Business Administration, 2005.

Capaldo, G., and M. Fontes. "Support for Graduate Entrepreneurs in New Technology-Based Firms: An Exploratory Study from Southern Europe." *Enterprise and Innovation Management Studies* 2, no. 1 (2001): 65–78.

Cardon, M. S., M. Foo, D. Shepherd, and J. Wiklund. "Exploring the Heart: Emotion Is a Hot Topic." *Entrepreneurship Theory and Practice* 36, no. 1 (2012): 1–11.

Carland, James W., Hoy Frank, William R. Boulton, and Jo Ann C. Carland. "Differentiating Entrepreneurs from Small Business Owners: A Conceptualization." *Academy of Management Review* 9, (1994): 354–359.

Carlsson, B., P. Braunerhjelm, M. McKkelvey, C. Olofsson, L. Persson, and H. Ylinenpaa. "The Evolving Domain of Entrepreneurship Research, *Small Business Economics* 41, no. 4 (2013): 913–930.

Carree, M. A, and A. R. Thurik. "The Impact of Entrepreneurship on Economic Growth." In *Handbook of Entrepreneurship Research*, 437–471. 2003.

Carter, N. M., W. B. Gartner, and P. D. Reynolds. "Exploring Start-Up Event Sequences," *Journal of Business Venturing* 11, no. 1 (1996): 51–66.

Casson, M. *The Entrepreneur: An Economic Theory.* 2nd ed. Cheltenham, UK: Edward Elgar, 2003.

Cassar, G. "The Financing of Business Start-Ups." *Journal of Business Venturing* 19, no. 2 (2004): 261–283.

Clark, Burton R. *Creating Entrepreneurial Universities—Organizational Pathways of Transformation.* Oxford: Elsevier Science, 1998.

Chell, E., J. Haworth, and S. Brearley. *The Entrepreneurial Personality: Concepts, Cases and Categories.* London: Routledge, 1991.

Chen, M. H. "Entrepreneurial Leadership and New Ventures: Creativity in Entrepreneurial Teams." *Creativity and Innovation Management* 16, no. 3 (2007): 239–249.

Chen, P. C., P. G. Greene, and A. Crick. "Does Entrepreneurial Self-Efficacy Distinguish Entrepreneurs from Managers?" *Journal of Business Venturing* 13, (1998): 295–316.

Chia, R. "Teaching Paradigm Shifting in Management Education: University Business Schools and the Entrepreneurial Imagination." *Journal of Management Studies* 33, no. 4 (1996): 40.

Christensen, C. M. *The Innovator's Dilemma: When New Technologies Cause Great Firms to fall.* Boston, Massachusetts: Harvard Business School Press, 1997.

Cockx, Raphael, Seven De Vocht, Jan Heylen, and Tom Van Bockstaele. *Encouraging Entrepreneurship in Europe: A Comparative Study Focused on Education,* Antwerpen: UFSIA, 2000.

Colette, Henry, France Hill, and Claire Leitch. "Entrepreneurship Education and Training: Can Entrepreneurship Be Taught? Part 1." *Education and Training* 47, (2005): 98–111.

Cooper, A. C., and Gascon, F. J. "Entrepreneurs, Processes of Founding, and New-Firm Performance." In *The State of the Art of Entrepreneurship,* 301–340.

————, and Timothy Folta. "Entrepreneurship and High Technology Clusters." In *The Blackwell Handbook of Entrepreneurship*, 349–367. 2000.

Cope, J. "Toward a Dynamic Learning Perspective of Entrepreneurship." *Entrepreneurship Theory and Practice* 29, no. 4 (2005): 373–397.

Corbett, A. C. "Learning Asymmetric and the Discovery of Entrepreneurial Opportunities." *Journal of Business Venturing* 22, no. 1 (2007): 97–118.

Covin, J., and D. Slevin. "New Venture Strategic Posture, Structure and Performance: An Industry Life Cycle Analysis." *Journal of Business Venturing* 5, (1990): 123–135.

Cowling, M., and M. Taylor. "Entrepreneurial Women and Men: Two Different Species?" *Small Business Economics* 16, no. 3 (2001): 167–175.

Cox, L. W., S. I. Mueller, and S. E. Moss. "The Impact of Entrepreneurship Education on Entrepreneurial Self-Efficacy." *International Journal of Entrepreneurship Education* 1, no. 2 (2003): 229–247.

Cromie, S., I. Callaghan, and M. Jansen. "The Entrepreneurial Tendencies of Managers: A Research Note." *British Journal of Management* 3, (1992): 1–5.

Craid, S. "The Entrepreneurial Tendency of Occupational Group." *International Small Business Journal* 9, (1991): 75–81.

————. "What Does It Mean to Be Entrepreneurial?" *British Journal of Management* 1, (1990): 137–145.

Crant, J. M. "The Proactive Personality Scale as a Predictor of Entrepreneurial Intentions." *Journal of Small Business Management* 34, no. 3 (1996): 42–49.

Cromie, S., and J. O'Donoghue. "Assessing Entrepreneurial Inclinations." *International Small Business Journal* 10, no. 2 (1992): 66–73.

————. "Assessing Entrepreneurial Inclinations: Some Approaches and Empirical Evidence." *European Journal of Work and Organizational Psychology* 9, no. 1 (2000): 7–30.

————. "Assessing Entrepreneurial Implications: Some Approaches and Empirical Evidence." *European Journal of Work and Organizational Psychology* 9, no. 1 (2000): 7–30.

Cunningham, J. B., and J. Lischeron. "Defining Entrepreneurship." *Journal of Small Business Management* 29, no. 1 (1991): 45–61.

Curran, J. "What Is Small Business Policy in the UK For? Evaluation and Assessing Small Business Policies." *International Business Journal*, (2000).

————, and R. Blackburn. *Researching the Small Enterprise*. London: Sage, 2000.

Daily, C., and D. R. Dalton. "Financial Performance of Founder-Managed versus Professionally Managed Small Corporations." *Journal of Small Business Management* 30, no. 2 (1992): 25–34.

Davey, T., P. Hannon, and A. Penaluna. "Entrepreneurship Education and the Role of Universities in Entrepreneurship." *Industry and Higher Education* 30, no. 3 (2016): 171–182.

Davidsson, P. (2004). Researching entrepreneurship, Springer, New York.

————, L. Achenhagen, and L. Naldi. "Small Firm Growth." *Foundation and Trends in Entrepreneurship* 6, no. 2 (2010): 98–166.

————, F. Delmar, and J. Wiklund. "Entrepreneurship as Growth: Growth as Entrepreneurship." In *Strategic Entrepreneurship*, edited by M. Hilt and D. Ireland. Oxford: Blackwell, 2002.

————. "Culture, Structure and Regional Levels of Entrepreneurship." *Entrepreneurship and Regional Development* 7, no. 1, (1995): 41–62.

————, Fredrick Delmar, and Johan Wiklund. "Entrepreneurship as Growth: Growth as Entrepreneurship." In *Strategic Entrepreneurship*: *Creating a New Mindset*, 328–342. 2002.

Day, D. L., "Research Linkages between Entrepreneurship and Strategic Management or General Management." In *The State of the Art of Entrepreneurship*, 117–163. 1992.

Deakins, D. *Entrepreneurship and Small Firms*. New York: McGraw Hill, 1996.

————, and M. Freel. "Entrepreneurial Learning and the Growth Process in SMEs." *The Learning Organization* 5, no. 3 (1998): 144–155.

Deeds, David L., Donna DeCarolis, and James Coombs. "Firm-Specific: Resources and Wealth Creation in High-Technology Ventures: Evidence from Newly Public Biotechnology Firms." *Entrepreneurship Theory and Practice* 22, (1998): 55–3.

Delmar, Fredrick, P. Davidsson, and William Gartner. "Arriving at the High-Growth Firm." *Journal of Business Venturing* 18, (2003): 189–216.

Deschoolmeester D., T. Schamp, A. M. Vandenbroucke, and K. Leger. "The Influence of Management Training on the Entrepreneurial Attitudes and Managerial Techniques of Small Business Starters (SMEs)." (1997).

DeTienne, D., and K. Wennberg. "Studying Exit from Entrepreneurship: New Directions and Insights." *International Small Business Journal* 34, no. 20 (2016): 151–156.

Dilts, J. C., and S. M. Fowler. "Internships: Preparing Students for an Entrepreneurial Career." *Journal of Business and Entrepreneurship* 11, no. 1 (1999): 51–63.

Drucker, Peter. "The Discipline of Innovation." *Harvard Business Review*, August 1, 2002.

Duggan, R. "Promoting Innovation in Industry, Government and Higher Education." *Journal of Long Range Planning* 29, no. 4 (1996): 503–513.

Duncan, Joseph W., and Douglas P. Handler. "The Misunderstood Role of Small Business." *Business Economics* 29, (1994): 1–6.

Duval-Couetil, N. "Assessing the Impact of Entrepreneurship Education Programs: Challenges and Approaches." *Journal of Small Business Management* 51, no. 3 (2013): 394–409.

Eckhardt, J., and S. Shane. "Opportunities and Entrepreneurship." *Journal of Management* 29, no. 3 (2003): 333–349.

Erkkila, K. *Entrepreneurial Education*. New York: Carland, 2000.

Etzkowitz, H. "The Norms of Entrepreneurial Science: Cognitive Effects of the New University-Industry Linkages." *Research Policy* 27, no. 8 (1998): 823–833.

Fayolle, A. "Evaluation of Entrepreneurship Education: Behavior Performing or Intention Increasing." *International Journal of Entrepreneurship and Small Business* 2, no. 1 (2005): 89–98.

———. *Handbook of Research on Small Business and Entrepreneurship.* Cheltenham: Edward Elgar, 2014.

———, P. Kyro, and J. M. Ulijn. *Entrepreneurship Research in Europe: Perspectives and Outcomes.* Cheltenham: Edward Elgar, 2005.

Fiet, J. O. "Theoretical Side of Teaching Entrepreneurship." *Journal of Business Venturing* 16, (2000): 1–24.

———. "The Pedagogical Side of Teaching Entrepreneurship." *Journal of Business Venturing* 16, no. 2 (2001): 101–117.

Finkle, T., and D. Deeds. "Trends in the Market for Entrepreneurship Faculty, 1989–1998." *Journal of Business Venturing* 16, no. 6 (2001): 613–631.

Fleming, P. "The Role of Structured Interventions in Shaping Graduates Entrepreneurship." In *Internationalizing Entrepreneurship Education and Training.* 1993

Fuller, E. *Small Business Trends, Some Implications for Skills and Training into the Next Century.* United Kingdom: Skills and Enterprises Network, 1993.

Fuller-Love, N. "Management Development in Small Firms." *International Journal of Management Reviews* 8, no. 3 (2006): 175–190.

Garavan, T. N., and B. O'Cinneide. "Entrepreneurship Education and Training Programs: A Review and Evaluation, Part 1." *Journal of Industrial Training* 18, no. 8 (1994): 3–12.

Gartner, William B., and Karl H. Vesper. "Experiments in Entrepreneurship Education Successes and Failures." *Journal of Small Business Venturing* 9, (1994): 179–187.

———. "A Conceptual Framework for Describing the Phenomenon of New Venture Creation." *Academy of Management Review* 10, (1985): 696–706.

———, B. J. Bird, and J. A. Starr. "Differentiating Entrepreneurial from Organizational Behavior." *Entrepreneurship Theory and Practice* 16, no. 3 (1992): 13–31.

———. "What Are We Talking about When We Talk about Entrepreneurship?" *Journal of Business Venturing* 5, (1990): 15–28.

Giamartino, G. A., P. P. McDougal, and B. J. Bird. "International Entrepreneurship: The State of the Field." *Entrepreneurship Theory and Practice* 18, no. 1 (1993): 37–42.

Gibb, A. A. "Entrepreneurship and Small Management: Can We Afford to Neglect Them in the Twenty-First Century Business School?" *British Journal of Management* 7, no. 4 (1996): 309–324.

———. "Enterprise Culture and Education: Understanding Enterprise Education and Its Links with Small Business Entrepreneurships and Wilder Educational Goals." *International Small Business Management Journal* 11, no. 3 (1993): 11–24.

———. "In Pursuit of a New 'Enterprise' and 'Entrepreneurship' Paradigm for Learning: Creative Deconstruction, New Values, New Ways of Doing Things and New Combination of Knowledge." *International Journal of Management Review* 4, no. 3 (2002): 213–231.

Gorman, G., D. Hanlon, and K. Wayne. "Some Research Perspectives on Entrepreneurship Education, Enterprise Education and Education for Small Business Management: A Ten-Year Literature Review." *International Small Business Journal,* (1997): 56–77.

Grant, Alan. "Entrepreneurship—the Major Academic Discipline for the Business Education Curriculum for the 21st Century." In *Education Entrepreneurship for Wealth Creation*, edited by M. G. Scott, P. Rosa, and H. Klandet, 16–28. Lyme, USA: Ashgate, 1998.

Greene, P., J. Katz, and B. Johannisson. "From the Guest Co-Editors: Entrepreneurship Education." *Academy of Management Learning and Education* 3, no. 3 (2004): 238–41.

Greer, C.R. *Strategic Human Resources Management: A General Managerial Approach*. Upper Saddle River, New Jersey: Prentice Hall, 2001.

Gries, T., and W. Naude. "Entrepreneurship and Structural Economic Transformation." *Small Business Economics* 34, (2010): 13–29.

Gulati, R. N., N. Nohria, and A. Zaheer. "Strategic Network." *Strategic Management Journal* 21, no. 3 (2000): 203–16.

Hall, J., and C. W. Hofer. "Venture Capitalists' Decision Criteria in New Venture Evaluation." *Journal of Business Venturing* 8, no. 1: (1993): 25–42.

Hamel, Gary. "Bringing Silicon Valley Inside." *Harvard Business Review.* May 1, 2000.

Hanks, Steven H., C. J. Watson, E. Jansen, and Gaylen N. Chandler. "Tightening the Life-Cycle Construct: A Taxonomic Study of Growth Stage Configurations in High-Technology Organizations." *Entrepreneurship Theory and Practice* 18, (1993): 5–29.

Hansemark, O. C. "The Effects of an Entrepreneurship Program on Need for Achievement and Locus Control of Reinforcement." *International Journal of Entrepreneurial Behavior and Research* 4, no. 1 (1998): 28–50.

Harrison, R. T., C. M. Leitch, and M. McAdam. "Breaking Glass: Towards a Gendered Analysis of Entrepreneurial Leadership." *Journal of Small Business Management,* (2015).

———, and C. M. Leitch. "Entrepreneurship and Leadership: The Implications for Education and Development." *Entrepreneurship and Regional Development* 6, no. 2 (1994): 111–25.

Hellmann, T. "Entrepreneurs and the Process of Obtaining Resources." *Journal of Economics and Management Strategy* 16, no. 1 (2007): 81–109.

Henry J., and D. Walker. *Managing Innovation.* Sage, 1992.

Hisrich R. D., and M. P. Peter. *Entrepreneurship: Starting, Developing and Managing a New Enterprise.* 3rd ed. Irwin, 1995.

Hitt, M. A., R. D. Ireland, M. Camp, D. G. Sirmon, and C. A. Trahms. "Strategic Entrepreneurship: Creating Value for Individuals, Organizations, and Society." *Academy of Perspectives,* (2011): 57–75.

Holtz-Eakin, D., D. Joulfaian, and H. S. Rosen. "Entrepreneurial Decisions and Liquidity Constraints." *Rand Journal of Economics* 25, (1994): 334–347.

———, D. D. Joulfaian, and H. S. Rosen. "Sticking It Out: Entrepreneurial Survival and Liquidity Constraints." *Journal of Political Economy* 102, (1994): 53–75.

Honig, B. "Entrepreneurship Education: Toward a Model of Contingency-Based Business Planning." *Academy of Management Learning and Education* 3, no. 3 (2004): 258–73.

Hornaday, R. W. "Thinking about Entrepreneurship." *Journal of Small Business Management* 30, no. 4 (1992): 12–23.

Hoy, Frank, Patricia P. McDougal, and Derrik E. D'Souza. "Strategies and Environments of High-Growth Firms." In *The State of the Art of Entrepreneurship.* 1992.

Hsu, D. K., J. Wiklund, S. E. Anderson, and B. S. Coffey. "Entrepreneurial Exit Intentions and the Business-Family Interface." *Journal of Business Venturing*, (2016).

Hynes, B. "Entrepreneurship Education and Training: Introducing Entrepreneurship into Non-Business Disciplines." *Journal of European Industrial Training* 20, no. 8 (1996): 8–10.

Hytti, U., and P. Kuopusjarvi. *Evaluating and Measuring Entrepreneurship and Enterprise Education Methods, Tools and Practices.* 2004.

Interman. *Profiles of Entrepreneurship Development Programs,* Geneva: International Labor Office, 1991.

Jack, S. L., and A. R. Anderson. "Entrepreneurship Education within Enterprise Culture." *International Journal of Entrepreneurial Behavior and Research* 5, no. 3 (1999): 110.

Johannisson, B. "University Training for Entrepreneurship: Swedish Approaches." *Entrepreneurship and Regional Development* 3, no. 1 (1991): 67–82.

Jones-Evans, D. "Technical Entrepreneurship, Experience and the Management of Small Technology-Based Firms." *Entrepreneurship and Regional Development* 9, no. 1 (1997): 65–90.

Kantor, R. M., and L. Richardson. "Engines of Progress: Designing and Running Entrepreneurial Vehicles in Established Companies." *Journal of Business Venturing* 6, (1991): 209–229.

———, J. North, A. P. Bernstein, and A. Williamson. "Engines of Progress: Designing and Running Entrepreneurial Vehicles in Established Companies." *Journal of Business Venturing* 5, (1990): 415–430.

Kao, R. W. *An Entrepreneurship Approach to Corporate Management.* London: Prentice Hall, 1997.

Kao, J. *The Entrepreneurial Organization.* London: Prentice Hall, 1991.

Katz, J. A. "The Institution and Infrastructure of Entrepreneurship." Entrepreneurship Theory and Practice, (Spring 1991): 85.

Kazanjian, R. K. "Relation of Dominant Problems to Stages of Growth in Technology-Based New Ventures." *Academy of Management Journal* 31, no. 2 (1988): 257–282.

———, and R. Drazin. "A State-Contingent Model of Design and Growth for Technology-Based New Ventures." *Journal of Business Venturing* 5, no. 3 (1990): 137–150.

Keen, P. G. W., and E. M. Knapp *Every Manager's Guide to Business Processes.* Boston: Harvard Business School Press, 1996.

Kent, C. *Entrepreneurship Education: Current Development, Future Directions.* New York: Quorum Books, 1990.

Kempster, S., and J. Cope. "Learning to Lead in the Entrepreneurial Context." *International Behavior and Research* 16, no. 1 (2010): 5–34.

Kerr, W. R., and R. Nanda. "Financing Constraints and Entrepreneurship." In *Handbook of Research on Innovation and Entrepreneurship.* Cheltenham, UK: Edward Elgar Publishing, 2011.

King, R. G., and R. Levine. "Finance, Entrepreneurship, and Growth: Theory and Evidence." *Journal of Monetary Economics* 32, (1993): 513–542.

Kirby, D. A. "Management Education and Small Business Development: An Exploratory Study of Small Firms in the

UK." *Journal of Small Business Management* 28, no.4 (1990): 78–87.

———, and D. Mullen. "Developing Enterprising Undergraduates." *Journal of European Industrial Training* 14, no. 2 (1990): 27–32.

———. "Developing Graduate Entrepreneurs: The UK Graduate Enterprise Program." *Entrepreneurship, Innovation and Change* 1, no. 2 (1992): 165–75.

———. "Entrepreneurship Education: Can Business Schools Meet the Challenge?" *Education and Training* 46, no. 8–9 (2004): 510–19.

———. *Entrepreneurship*, Maidenhead: McGraw Hill, 2003.

Kirzner, I. M. "The Alert and Creative Entrepreneur: A Clarification." *Small Business Economics* 32, no. 2 (2009): 145–152.

Klapper, L., R. Amit, and M. F. Guillen. "Entrepreneurship and Firm Formation across Countries." In *International Differences in Entrepreneurship*. Chicago, Illinois: University of Chicago Press, 2010.

Kolvereid, L. "Prediction of Employment Status Choice Intentions." *Entrepreneurship Theory and Practice* 20, no. 3 (1996): 47–57.

———, and O. Moen. "Entrepreneurship among Business Graduates: Does a Major in Entrepreneurship Make a Difference?" *Journal of European Industrial Training* 21, no. 4 (1997): 154–60.

Kourilsky, M. L. "Entrepreneurial Thinking and Behavior: What Role in the Classroom?" In *Entrepreneurship Education: Current Developments, Future Directions*, 137–152. Quorum Books, 1990.

———. "Entrepreneurship Education: Opportunity in Search of Curriculum." *Business Education Forum* 50, (1995): 11–15.

Krueger, N. F., and A. L. Carsrud. "Entrepreneurial Intentions: Applying the Theory of Planned Behavior." *Entrepreneurship and Regional Development* 5, (1993): 315–30.

———, M.D. Reilly, and A. L. Carsud. "Competing Models of Entrepreneurial Intentions." *Journal of Business Venturing* 15, no. 5–6 (2000): 411–32.

Kuratko, D. F. "Entrepreneurial Leadership in the 21st Century." *Journal of Leadership and Organizational Studies* 13, no. 4 (2007): 1–12.

————, and R. M. Hodgetts. *Entrepreneurship: A Contemporary Approach*. 2nd ed. Fort Worth, USA: Dryden, 1992.

————, J. S. Hornsby, D. W. Naffziger, and R. V. Montagno. "Implementing Entrepreneurial Thinking in Established Organizations." *Advanced Management Journal*, (1993): 28–33.

————. "The Real Challenges Are Risk, Stress, Ego, and Motivations." *Entrepreneurship, Innovation, and Change* 4, no.1 (1995): 3–10.

————. "The Emergence of Entrepreneurship Education: Developments, Trends and Challenges." *Entrepreneurship Theory and Practice* 29, no. 5 (2005): 577–97.

Laukkanen, M. "Exploring Alternative Approaches in High-Level Entrepreneurship Education: Creation Micro Mechanism for Endogenous Regional Growth." *Journal of Entrepreneurship and Regional Development* 12, (2000): 25–47.

Leitch, C. M., C. McMullan, and R. T. Harrison. "The Development of Entrepreneurial Leadership: The Role of Human, Social and Institutional Capital." *British Journal of Management* 24, no. 3 (2013): 347–366.

————, and T. Vollery. "Entrepreneurial Leadership: Insights and Directions." *International Small Business Journal* 35, no. 2 (2017): 147–156.

————, and R. T. Harrison. "A Process Model for Entrepreneurship Education and Development." *International Journal of Entrepreneurial Behavior and Research* 5, no. 3 (1999): 8–10.

Levie, J. *A Survey on Entrepreneurship Education in Higher Education in England*. London: London Business School, 1999.

Lichtenstein, B. M., N. M. Carter, K. J. Dooley, and W. B. Gartner. "Complexity Dynamic of Nascent Entrepreneurship." *Journal of Business Venturing* 22, no. 3 (2007): 238–61.

Lowe, R. A., and A. Ziedonis. "Over-Optimism and the Performance of Entrepreneurial Firms." *Management Science* 52, no. 2 (2006): 173–186.

Lumpkin, G. T., and G. G. Dess. "Clarifying the Entrepreneurial Orientation Construct and Linking It to Performance." *Academy of Management Review* 21, no. 1 (1996): 135–72.

Lundstrom, A., and L. A. Stevenson. *Entrepreneurship Policy: Theory and Practice.* Springer, 2005.

Luthje, C., and N. Kranke. "The Making of an Entrepreneur: Testing a Model of Entrepreneurial Intent among Engineering Students at MIT." *R and D Management* 33, no. 2 (2003): 135–47.

Lyles, M. A., I. S. Bird, B. Orris, and D. F. Kuratko. "Formalized Planning in Small Business: Increasing Strategic Choices." *Journal of Small Business Management* 31, no. 2 (1993): 38–50.

MacKenzie, L. R. "Fostering Entrepreneurship as a Rural Economic Development Strategy." *Economic Development Review* 10, no. 4 (1993): 38–44.

Marshall. J. N., N. Alderman, C. Wong, and A. Thwaites. "The Impact of Management Training and Development on Small and Medium-Sized Enterprises." *International Small Business Journal* 13, no. 4 (1995): 73–90.

Martinelli, A. "Entrepreneurship and Management." In *Handbook of Economic Sociology*, 476–503. 1994.

Mathews, C. H., and S. G. Scott. "Uncertainty and Planning in Small and Entrepreneurial Firms: An Empirical Assessment." *Journal of Small Business Management* 33, no. 4 (1995): 34–52.

Matlay, Harry, and Jay Mitra. Entrepreneurship and Learning: The Double Act in The Triple Helix." *International Journal of Entrepreneurship and Innovation* 3, no. 1 (2002): 7–16.

McCarthy, A. M., F. D. Schoorman, and A. C. Cooper. "Reinvestment Decisions by Entrepreneurs: Rational Decision-Making of Escalation of Commitment?" *Journal of Business Venturing* 8, no. 1 (1993): 9–24.

McGrath, R. G., and I. C. MacMillan. *The Entrepreneurial Mindset.* Boston: Harvard Business School Publishing, 2000.

———, and I. C. MacMillan. "Discovery Driven Planning." *Harvard Business Review*, 1995.

McGuirk, Helen, Helena Lenihan, and Mark Hart. "Measuring the Impact of Innovative Human Capital on Small Firms' Propensity to Innovate." *Research Policy* 44, no. 4 (2015): 965–76.

McMillan, J., and C. Woodruff. "The Central Role of Entrepreneurs in Transition Economies." *Journal of Economic Perspectives* 16, (2002): 153–170.

Merz, G. R., P. B. Weber, and V. B. Laetz. "Linking Small Business Management with Entrepreneurial Growth." *Journal of Small Business Management* 32, no. 4 (October 1994): 48–60.

Messersmith, G. J., and J. W. Wales. "Entrepreneurial Orientation and Performance in Young Firms: The Role of Human Resources Management." *International Small Business Journal* 31, no. 2 (2011): 115–136.

Miller, K. D. "Risk and Rationality in Entrepreneurial Process." *Strategic Entrepreneurship Journal* 1, no. 1–2 (2007): 57–74.

Milton, D. G. "The Complete Entrepreneur." *Entrepreneurship: Theory and Practice* 13, (1989): 9–19.

Miner, J. B. *A Psychological Typology of Successful Entrepreneur.* London: Quorum Books, 1997.

Minniti, M., and W. D. Bygrave. The Micro-Foundations of Entrepreneurship." *Entrepreneurship: Theory and Practice* 23, no. 4 (1999): 41–52.

Monsted, M. "Strategic Alliance as an Analytical Perspective for Innovative SMEs." In *New Technology-Based Firms in the 1990s,* 99–111. London: Paul Chapman, 1998.

Morris, M. H., P. Jones, and D. Nel. "The Informal Sector, Entrepreneurship, and Economic Development." *Journal of Developmental Entrepreneurship* 2, no. 2 (1997): 83–98.

Mueller, S. L., and A. S. Thomas. "Culture and Entrepreneurial Potential: A Nine-Country Study of Locus of Control and Innovativeness." *Journal of Business Venturing* 16, (2000): 51–75.

Neck, H. M., and P. G. Greene. "Entrepreneurship Education: Known Worlds and New Frontiers." *Journal of Small Business Management* 49, no. 1 (2011): 55–70.

Nonaka, I., and H. Takeuchi. *The Knowledge-Creating Company.* New York: Oxford University Press, 1995.

Nystrom, H. *Creativity and Entrepreneurship.* London: Sage Publications, 1995.

Ohe, T., S. Honjo, and D. B. Merrifield. "Japanese Corporate Ventures: Success Curve." *Journal of Business Venturing* 7, (1992): 171–180.

Olson, P. D. "Entrepreneurship: Process and Abilities." *Entrepreneurship Theory and Practice* 10, no. 1 (1995): 25–32.

———, and D. Bosserman. "Attributes of the Entrepreneurial Type." *Business Horizons* (May–June 1984): 53–6.

———, and D. W. Bokor. "Strategy Process-Content Interaction: Effects on Growth Performance in Small, Start-Up Firms." *Journal of Small Business Management* 33, no. 1 (1995): 34–44.

Parker, S. C. *The Economics of Entrepreneurship*. Cambridge, UK: Cambridge University Press, 2009.

Peterman, N. E., and J. Kennedy. "Enterprise Education: Influencing Students Perceptions of Entrepreneurship." *Entrepreneurship Theory and Practice* 28, no. 2 (2003): 129–44.

Pickle, H. B., and R. L. Abrahamson. *Small Business Management*. 5th ed. New York: John Wiley, 1990.

Plaschka, G. R., and H. P. Welsch. "Emerging Structure in Entrepreneurship Education: Curriculum Designs and Strategies." *Entrepreneurship Theory and Practice* 14, no. 3 (1990): 55–70.

Porter, I. "The Relation of Entrepreneurship Education to Business Education." *Simulation and Gaming* 25, no. 3 (1994): 416–420.

Porter, Michael E. "Strategy and the Internet." *Harvard Business Review*, 2001.

Quadrini, V. "The Importance of Entrepreneurship for Wealth Concentration and Mobility." *Review of Income and Wealth* 45, (1999): 1–19.

Quadrini, V. "Entrepreneurship, Saving and Social Mobility." Review of Economic Dynamics 3, (2000): 1–40.

Rae, D., and M. Carswell. "Using a Life-Story Approach in Researching Entrepreneurial Learning: The Development of a Conceptual Model and Its Implication in the Design of Learning Experiences." *Education and Training* 42, no. 4/5 (2000): 220–28(9).

Ray, D. M. "Understanding the Entrepreneur: Entrepreneurial Attributes, Experience and Skills." *Entrepreneurship and Regional Development* 5, (1993): 345–57.

Renko, M., A. El Tarabishy, A. I. Carsrud, and M. Brannback. "Understanding and Measuring Entrepreneurial Leadership." *Journal of Small Business Management* 53, no. 1 (2015): 54–74.

Reynolds, P. D. "Sociology and Entrepreneurship Concepts and Contributions." *Entrepreneurship, Theory and Practice* 16, no. 2 (1991): 47–67.

———. "New and Small Firms in Expanding Markets." *Small Business Economics* 9, no. 1 (1997): 79–84.

———, and Sammis White. *The Entrepreneurial Process: Economic Growth, Men, Women, and Minorities.* Westport, Connecticut: Quorum Books, 1997.

Risker, D. C. "Toward an Innovation Typology of Entrepreneurs." *Journal of Small Business and Entrepreneurship* 15, no. 2 (1998): 27–41.

Roberts, Edward B. *Entrepreneurs in High Technology,* New York, New York: Oxford University Press, (1991).

———. "The Technological Base of the New Enterprise." *Research Policy* 29, (1991): 283–298.

Roberts, R. *Finance for Small and Entrepreneurial Business.* London and New York: Routledge, 2015.

Robinson, P., and E. Sexton. "The Effect of Education and Experience Self-Employment Success." *Journal of Business Venturing* 9, no. 2 (1994): 141–57.

———, and M. Haynes. "Entrepreneurship Education in America's Major Universities." *Entrepreneurship: Theory and Practice,* (Spring 1991): 41–51.

———, D. V. Simpton, J. C. Huefner, and H. K. Hunt. "An Attitude Approach to the Prediction of Entrepreneurs." *Entrepreneurship: Theory and Practice* 15, no. 4 (1992): 13–31.

Roomi, M. A., and P. Harrison. "Entrepreneurial Leadership: What Is It and How Should It Be Taught?" *International Review of Entrepreneurship* 9, no. 3 (2011): 1–43.

Rosa, P., M. G. Scott, and H. Klandt. *Educating Entrepreneurs in Modernizing Economices.* Stirling Management Series. England/ USA: Avebury, 1996.

Rupert, A. E. *Entrepreneurship and Economic Growth.* Pretoria: HSRRC Publishers, 1994.

Sandberg, W. "Strategic Management's Potential Contributions to a Theory of Entrepreneurship." *Entrepreneurship Theory and Practice* 16, no. 3 (1992): 73–90.

Sahlman, W. A., and H. H. Stevenson. *The Entrepreneurial Venture.* Boston, Massachusetts: Harvard Business School Publications, 1992.

Schmitz, H. "Collective Efficiency: Growth Path for Small-Scale Industry." *Journal of Development Studies* 31, (1995): 49–128.

Schroeder, Dean M. "A Dynamic Perspective on the Impact of Process Innovation upon Competitive Strategies." *Strategic Management Journal* 2, (1990): 25–41.

Scott, M. G., P. Rosa, and H. Klandt. *Educating Entrepreneurs for Wealth Creation,* edited by M. G. Scott, P. Rosa, and H. Klandt. 1998.

Sexenian, A. *Regional Advantage: Culture and Competition in Silicon Valley and Rote 128.* Cambridge: Harvard University Press, 1994.

Sexton, D., and N. Nowman-Upton. *Entrepreneurship: Creative and Growth.* New York: MacMillan Publishing, 1991.

Shan, W. "An Empirical Analysis of Organizational Strategies by Entrepreneurial High-Technology Firms." *Strategic Management Journal* 11, no. 2 (1990): 129–139.

Shane, S. *A General Theory of Entrepreneurship: The Individual-Opportunity Nexus.* Cheltenham, UK: Edward Elgar, 2003.

Sarason, Y., T. Dean, and J. F. Dillard. "Entrepreneurship as the Nexus of Individual and Opportunity: A Structuration View." *Journal of Business Venturing* 21, no. 3 (2006): 286.

Savaer, K. G., and L. R. Scott. "Person, Process, Choice: The Psychology of the New Venture Creation." *Entrepreneurship Theory and Practice* 16, no. 1 (1991): 23–45.

Sheehan, M. "Human Resource Management and Performance: Evidence from Small and Medium-Sized Firms." *International Small Business Journal* 32, no. 5 (2014): 545–570.

Shepherd, D. A. "Educating Entrepreneurship Students about Emotion and Learning from Failure." *Academy of Management Learning and Education* 3, no. 3 (2004): 274–87.

Shook, K. G., R. L. Priem, and J. E. McGee. "Venture Creation and the Enterprising Individual: A Review and Synthesis." *Journal of Management* 29, no. 3 (2003): 379–99.

Slevin, D. P., and J. G. Covin. "Creating and Maintaining High Performance Teams." In *The State of the Art of Entrepreneurship*, 358–386. Boston, Massachusetts: PWS Kent Publishing Company, 1992.

Smeltzer, L. R., B. L. Van Hook, and R. W. Hutt. "Analysis of the Use of Advisors as Information Sources in Venture Start-Up." *Journal of Small Business Management* 29, no. 3 (1991): 10–19.

Smilor, R. W., and D. L. Sexton. *Leadership and Entrepreneurship*. Quorum Books, 1996.

Smith, Keith. "Innovation as a Systemic Phenomenon: Rethinking the Role of Policy." *Enterprise and Innovative Management Studies* 1, no. 1 2000: 73–102.

Solomon, G., and L. Fernald Jr. "Trends in Small Business Management and Entrepreneurship Education in the United States." *Entrepreneurship: Theory and Practice*, (1991): 25–40.

Sorrentino, M., and M. L. William. "Relatedness and Corporate Venturing: Does It Really Matter?" *Journal of Business Venturing* 19, (1995): 59–73.

Soriano, D. R., and J. M. C. Martinez. "Transmitting the Entrepreneurial Spirit to the Work Teams in SMEs: The Importance of Leadership." *Management Decision* 45, no. 7 (2007): 1102–1122.

Spilling, O. R. "Entrepreneurship in Cultural Perspective." *Entrepreneurship and Regional Development* 3, no. 1 (1991): 33–48.

Spinelli, Stephen, and Jeffry Timmons. *New Venture Creation for the 21st Century*. 6th ed. New York: McGraw Hill, 2003.

Spinosa, C., C. F. Florse, and H. L. Dreyfus. *Disclosing New World: Entrepreneurship, Democratic Action and the Cultivation of Solidarity*. Cambridge, Massachusetts: MIT Press, 1997.

Spulber, D. F. "Competition among Entrepreneurs." *Industrial and Corporate Change* 19, no. 1 (2010): 25–50.

———. "The Role of the Entrepreneur in Economic Growth." In *Handbook of Law, Innovation, and Growth*, 11–44. Northampton, Massachusetts: Edward Elgar, 2011.

Stanworth, J., and C. Gray. "Entrepreneurship and Education: Action-Based Research with Training Policy Implications in Britain." *International Small Business Journal* 10, no. 2 (1992): 11–23.

Stevenson, Howard H., and J. Carlos Jarillo. "A Paradigm of Entrepreneurship: Entrepreneurial Management." *Strategic Management Journal* 11, (1990): 17–27.

Stewart, W. H. *Psychological Correlates of Entrepreneurship*. New York: Garland Publishing, 1996.

Storey, D. J. *Understanding the Small Business Sector*. London and Boston, Massachusetts: International Thomson Business Press, 1994.

Sullivan, R. "Entrepreneurial Learning and Mentoring." *International Journal of Entrepreneurial Behavior and Research* 6, no. 3 (2000): 160–75.

Swedberg, Richard. "The Social Science View of Entrepreneurship: Introduction and Practical Application." In *Entrepreneurship, the Social Science View*, edited by Richard Swedberg, 7–44. Oxford Management Readers, Oxford: Oxford University Press, 2000.

Tate, C. E, J. F. Cox, F. Holy, V. Scarpello, and W. W. Stewart. *Small Business Management and Entrepreneurship*. Boston, USA: PWS Kent, 1992.

Teece, D. J. "Dynamic Capabilities: Routines versus Entrepreneurial Action." *Journal of Management Studies* 49, no. 8 (2012): 1395–1401.

Timmons, J. A., L. E. Smollen, and A. L. M. Dingee. *New Venture Creation: Entrepreneurship for the 21st Century*. 4th ed. Boston: Irwin, 1994.

————, and S. Spinnelli. *New Venture Creation: Entrepreneurship for the 21st Century*. New York: McGraw Hill, 2004.

Utsch, A., and A. Rauch. "Innovativeness and Initiative as Mediators between Achievement Orientation and Venture Performance." *Organizational Psychology* 9, no. 1 (2000): 45–62.

Utterback, James M. *Mastering the Dynamic of Innovation*. Harvard Business Press, 1996.

Van Clouse, G. H. "A Controlled Experiment Relating Entrepreneurial Education to Students' Start-Up Decisions." *Journal of Small Business Management* 28, no. 2 (1990): 45–53.

Van de Ven, A. "The Development of an Infrastructure for Entrepreneurship." *Journal of Business Venturing* 8, no. 3 (1993): 211–230.

Van Praag, C. M., and P. H. Versloot. "What Is the Value of Entrepreneurship? A Review of Research." *Small Business Economics* 29, (2007): 351–382.

Van Stel, A., M. Carree, and R. Thurik. "The Effect of Entrepreneurial Activity on National Economic Growth." *Small Business Economics* 24, (2005): 311–321.

Vesper, K. H. *New Venture Strategic*. Rev. ed. Englewood Cliffs: Prentice Hall, 1990.

————, and W. B. Gartner. "Measuring Progress in Entrepreneurship Education." *Journal of Business Venture* 12, no. 4 (1997): 403–21.

————, and W. B. Gartner. *University Entrepreneurship Program 1999*. Lloyd Greif Center for Entrepreneurial Studies, University of Southern California, 1999.

————. *Entrepreneurship Education*. Entrepreneurial Studies Center, University of California, 1993.

Vinnell, R., and T. Hamilton. "A Historical Perspective on Small Firm Development." *Entrepreneurship Theory and Practice* 23, (1999): 4–18.

Walter, S. G., and J. H. Block. "Outcomes of Entrepreneurship Education: An Institutional Perspective." *Journal of Business Venturing* 31, no. 2 (2016): 216–233.

Welsch, H. P., and J. R. Kickul. "Training for Successful Entrepreneurship Careers." In *Entrepreneurship Education: A Global View*. Aldershot: Ashgate, 2001.

Welter, F. "Contextualizing Entrepreneurship—Conceptual Challenges and Ways Forward." *Entrepreneurship Theory and Practice* 35, no. 1 (2011): 165–184.

Wennekers, A. R. M., and A. R. Thurik. "Linking Entrepreneurship and Economic Growth." *Small Business Economics* 13, (1999): 27–55.

Wiklund, Johan, P. Davidsson, and F. Delmar. "Expected Consequences of Growth and Their Effects on Growth Willingness in Different Samples of Small Firms." *Entrepreneurship Theory and Practice* 27, (2003): 247–269.

Williams, G. "2001: An Entrepreneurial Odyssey." *Entrepreneur* 27, no. 4 (1999): 106–113.

Whiting, B. G. "Creativity and Entrepreneurship: How Do They Relate?" *Journal of Creative Behavior* 22, no. 3 (1988): 178–83.

Wright, M., and I. Stigliani. "Entrepreneurship and Growth." *International Small Business Journal* 33, no. 1 (2013): 3–22.

Wyckham, R., and W. Wedley. "Factors Related to Venture Feasibility Analysis and Business Plan Preparation." *Journal of Small Business Management*, (1990).

Young, J. E. "Entrepreneurship Education and Learning for University Students and Practicing Entrepreneurs." In *Entrepreneurship 2000*, 215–238. Chicago, Illinois: Upstart Publishing, 1997.

Zahara, Shaker. A., and M. Wright. "Entrepreneurship's Next Act." *The Academy of Management Perspectives* 25, no. 4 (2011): 67–83.

———. "Predictors and Financial Outcomes of Corporate Entrepreneurship: An Exploratory Study." *Journal of Business Venturing* 6, (1991): 259–286.

———. "Environment, Corporate Entrepreneurship, and Financial Performance: A Taxonomy Approach." *Journal of Business venturing* 8, (1996): 319–340.

———, Duane R. Ireland, and Michael Hitt. "International Expansion, Technological Learning and New Venture

Performance." *Academy of Management Journal* 43, (2000): 925–950.

————, and James Hayton. "Technological Entrepreneurship: Current Debates and Emerging Research Issues." In *Crossroads of Entrepreneurship*, 185–207. 2004.

————, and Jeffrey G. Covin. "Business Strategy, Technology Policy and Company Performance." *Strategic Management Journal* 14, (1993): 451–478.

————, and William Bogner. "Technology Strategy and Software New Venture Performance: The Moderate Effect of the Competitive Environment." *Journal of Business Venturing* 15, (2000): 135–173.

SUBJECT INDEX

ABOUT THE AUTHOR

 Dan Vivek Nathan holds double master's degrees and professional postgraduate diploma in marketing management from the world-renowned The Chartered Institute of Marketing, UK. He has been previously working for groups of companies—Chesebrough-Pond's, EMI, Neiman Marcus, Blue Cross Blue Shield, and Sears, Roebuck and Company—and many other major retail companies. With over four decades of experience in marketing, market research, marketing research, statistics, information systems, customer relation management, and entrepreneurship, he has written the book *Global Market /Marketing Research in 21st Century and Beyond*. He is a recipient of 2021 CIM Fellowship badge/medal for his contribution toward marketing management.